THE SYNOPTIC GOSPELS
An Interpretation for Today

ROBIN COOPER

Hodder & Stoughton
LONDON SYDNEY AUCKLAND TORONTO

Acknowledgements

The publishers would like to thank Cambridge University Press for their permission to use the extracts from *The New English Bible* © 1970 Oxford and Cambridge University Presses.

British Library Cataloguing in Publication Data
Cooper, Robin, 1941–
  The synoptic gospels.
  1. Bible. N.T.   Synoptic Gospels – critical studies
  I. Title
  226.06

ISBN 0 340 49376 3

First published 1990

© 1990 Robin Cooper

All rights reserved. No part of this publication may be reproduced or transmitted in any form or by any means, electronic or mechanical, including photocopy, recording, or any information storage and retrieval system, without permission in writing from the publisher or under licence from the Copyright Licensing Agency Limited. Further details of such licenses (for reprographic reproduction) may be obtained from the Copyright Licensing Agency Limited, of 33–34 Alfred Place, London WC1E 7DP.

Typeset by Wearside Tradespools, Fulwell, Sunderland
Printed in Great Britain for the educational publishing division of Hodder and Stoughton Ltd, Mill Road, Dunton Green, Sevenoaks, Kent by Richard Clay Ltd, Bungay, Suffolk

To the
Rev. Geoffrey R. Tucker MA
with gratitude

Contents

Preface   vii

1   **The Background to the Synoptic Gospels**   1
     The political background at the time of Jesus   1
     The religious background at the time of Jesus   3
     Understanding the Synoptic Gospels   7
     The relationship between the Synoptic Gospels   9
     The Authorship and Date of the Synoptic Gospels   13
     The characteristics of the Synoptic Gospels   17

2   **The Birth Stories of Jesus**   21
     The differences between Matthew's and Luke's accounts   21
     The text of the birth stories   22
     The importance of the virgin birth for Christians today   25
     The importance of the birth of Jesus for Christians today   34

3   **Parables and their Meaning for Today**   37
     What is a parable?   37
     What is an allegory?   38
     Why did Jesus use parables?   38
     Some Lukan parables and their meaning for today   39
     The kingdom of heaven   45
     Some parables of the kingdom of heaven and their meaning for today   46

4   **The Miracles of Jesus in the Synoptic Gospels**   54
     What is a miracle?   54
     Did Jesus perform miracles?   55
     Why did Jesus heal people?   56
     The relationship between faith and miracle   56
     What is faith?   57
     The Church and healing today   57
     Exorcisms and their message for today   58
     Healing miracles and their message for today   63
     The importance of the healing miracles for Christians today: Summary   67
     Raising from the dead miracles and their message for today   68
     Nature miracles   70

5 **Responses to Jesus**   76
  The response of discipleship   76
  Discipleship today   77
  The response of the Jewish leaders: conflict stories and
    interpretations for today   79
  The response of the sinner and interpretations for today   87

6 **The Suffering and Death of Jesus**   91
  The narrative of Holy Week   91
  The importance of the Eucharistic words for Christians today   107
  What the Evangelists believe about the death of Jesus   117
  What the death of Jesus means for Christians today   117

7 **The Resurrection of Jesus in the Synoptic Gospels**   122
  What did the resurrection mean to the synoptic writers?   122
  What the resurrection means for Christians today   131

8 **Who is Jesus?**   136
  The major titles used of Jesus in the Synoptic Gospels   136
  Jesus: the Christ for today   140
  Jesus: the Son of God for today   146
  The title used by Jesus himself in the Synoptic Gospels   146
  Jesus: the Son of Man for today   151
  Other major titles used of Jesus   152
  Jesus: Saviour for today   152
  Jesus: Lord for today   153

Index of Gospel references   156

Preface

This book, which attempts to present a modern biblical approach to the Synoptic Gospels, is written for the classroom with special reference to those studying for GCSE examinations.

The book covers the main themes of the birth, life, death and resurrection of Jesus as portrayed in the three Gospels of Matthew, Mark and Luke, known as the Synoptic Gospels.

Obviously, in a book of this size, it has not been possible to include every interpretation of each event in the Gospels, but I have tried to encourage students to have an enquiring and critical approach to the Gospels and to ask themselves continually what relevance these Gospels have for today.

The book not only covers the text of the Gospels but also examines:

- the political and religious background to the time of Jesus;
- the purpose of the three authors and the characteristics of each Gospel;
- the influence of both the early Church and the authors on the traditions about Jesus; and
- the continual interpretation of the Gospels for Christians today.

In each chapter concerning the text of the Gospel, there are work sections which follow the assessment objectives required by the various examination boards for GCSE: knowledge, understanding and evaluation. There are suggestions for practical work and questions for examination practice.

All references quoted both from the Gospels and other biblical books are taken from the New English Bible. These quotes may be easily identified by this logo

Sections which discuss the application of the Gospels 'for today' are in italics and are, therefore, easily identifiable throughout the book.

I would like to thank my colleagues, Correna Dcaccia and Vincent Love for all their encouragement and advice, and Lucie, my wife, for all her help in preparing the typescript.

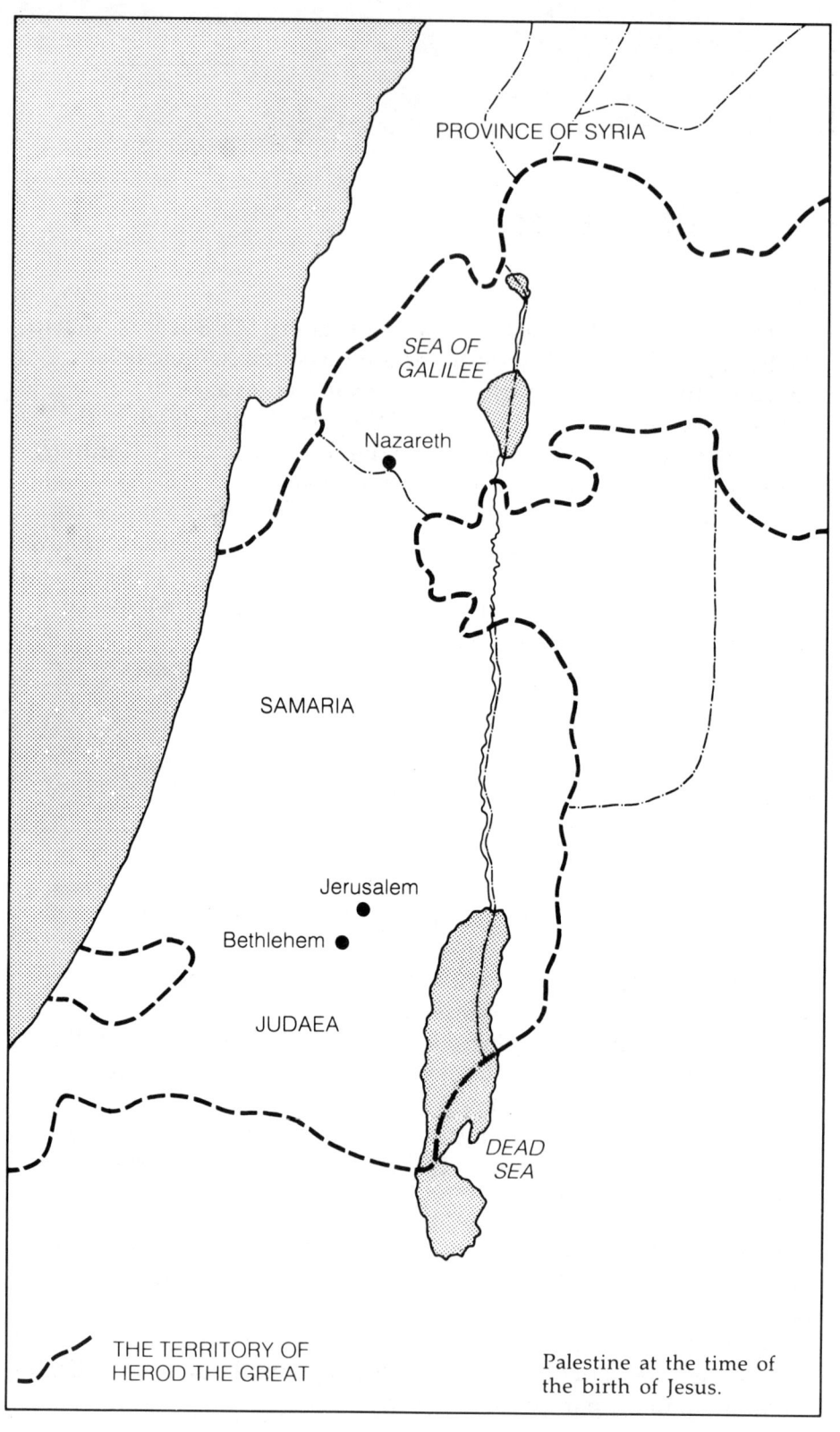
Palestine at the time of the birth of Jesus.

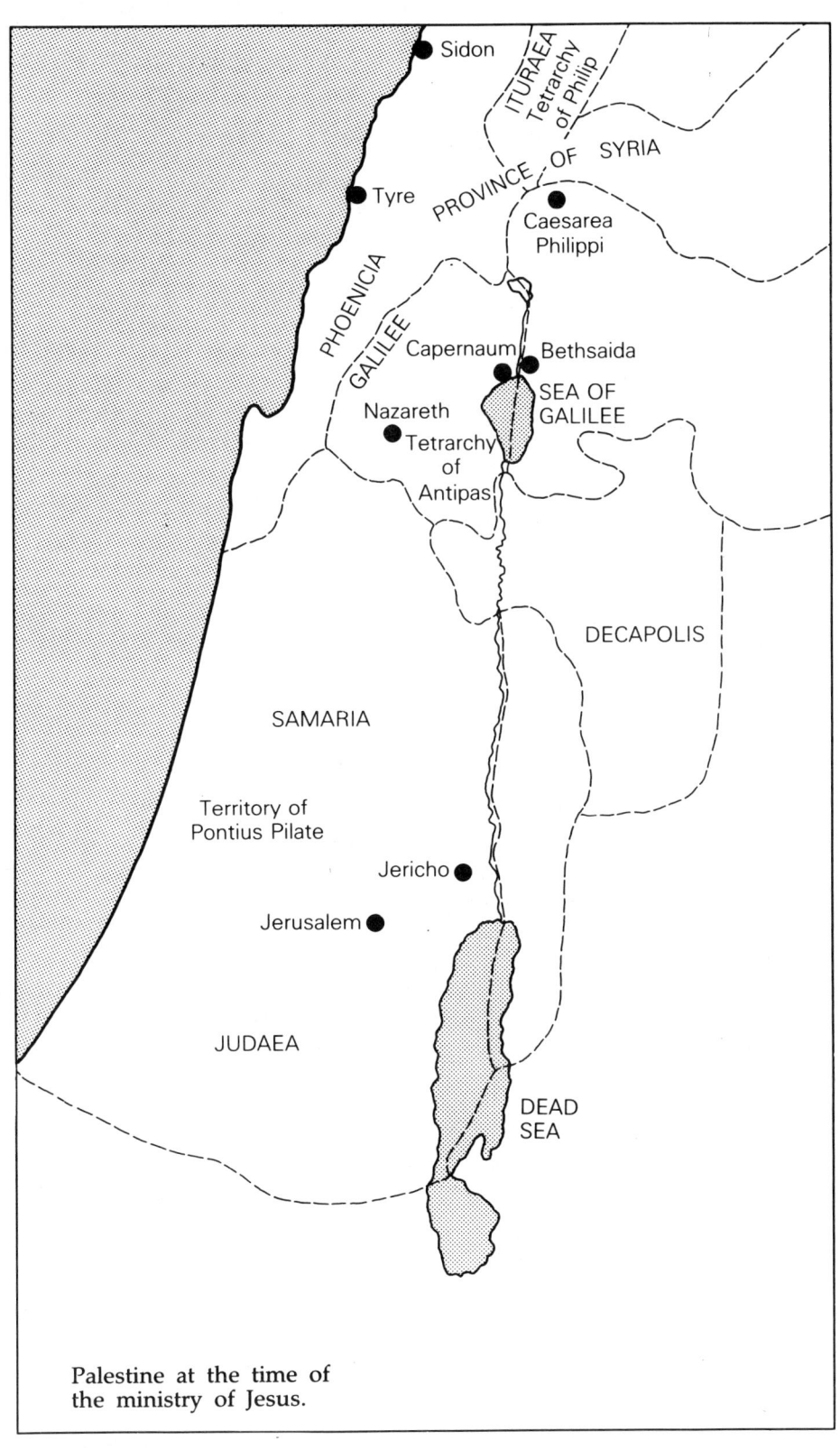
Palestine at the time of the ministry of Jesus.

1 The Background to the Synoptic Gospels

The Political Background at the Time of Jesus

Herod the Great

For a hundred years or so before the birth of Jesus, Palestine had been under the rule of the Romans.

At the time when Jesus was born, Herod the Great was the 'puppet king' who ruled Palestine for the Romans. He served Rome well but because of this he received hostile opposition from some Jews, especially the Pharisees.

The main reasons for this opposition were:

1. Herod was not a Jew. He came from Idumaea, to the south of Judaea. He had no real claim to any royal throne. He was regarded as a 'pretender', imposed on the Jewish nation by the Romans.
2. He showed little interest in Jewish law or customs. He provoked the Jews by promoting Greek culture and buildings in the holy city of Jerusalem.

Herod ruled from 37–4 BC. He was a clever man who brought an uneasy peace and stability to Palestine. He built new cities and was responsible for the building of the new Temple in Jerusalem.

Many people have condemned Herod as a cruel man and certainly he showed a cruel streak, especially towards his own family. His relationships were full of intrigue and conflict. He was passionately devoted to his second wife, Mariamne, but was equally capable of passionate jealousy. His mind was poisoned against her and her sons Aristobulus and Alexander. Convinced of her unfaithfulness, Herod had Mariamne executed in 29 BC and her sons in 7 BC. In 4 BC Antipater, son of his first wife Doris, was also executed shortly before Herod's own death in the same year.

On the death of Herod the Great, the Roman Emperor Augustus divided the kingdom among three of Herod's sons, Archelaus, Herod Antipas and Philip. However, they were not given the title of 'king' like their father.

- Archelaus was appointed ethnarch (a title similar to 'governor') of Judaea and Samaria;
- Herod Antipas, tetrarch (a title for a ruler who was not considered important enough to have the rank of king; again it amounted to being a 'governor') of Galilee.
- Philip, tetrarch of the lands of Ituraea and Trachonitis which was to the north east of the Sea of Galilee.

Archelaus was deposed in 6 AD and sent into exile. The territory of Judaea and Samaria was placed in the hands of a Roman Procurator (a Roman officer with the rank of governor). The most well-known procurator of Judaea and Samaria was Pontius Pilate 26–39 AD.

Herod Antipas

Herod Antipas was the ruler responsible for the death of John the Baptist. He had him killed after John had criticised Herod's marriage to Herodias, the wife of his half-brother Herod Philip (Luke 3:19).

This was the same Herod that Pontius Pilate sent the accused Jesus to during his trial, on the excuse that, because Jesus was a Galilean, he came under the rule of the Tetrarch of Galilee (Luke 23:2–7).

SUMMARY

- During the days of Herod the Great and his successors, Palestine was a troubled province of the Roman Empire. There was continual unrest.
- Most Jews hated the Romans, not only because they occupied the country by force but because they were also Gentiles (non-Jews).
- It was into this atmosphere that Jesus was born and grew up. In these troubled times Jesus conducted his ministry and was put to death.

The Religious Background at the Time of Jesus

The Sanhedrin

The Sanhedrin was the highest court of Jewish law. It dealt with all matters, both religious and political. The name 'Sanhedrin' means 'council'. The president of the council was the High Priest.

The origin of the Sanhedrin was the seventy men Moses appointed to assist him in judging the people of Israel. The seventy members of the Sanhedrin were drawn mainly from two opposing parties, the Sadducees and the Pharisees. In criminal cases the Sanhedrin could pass a sentence of death but could not carry out such a sentence without the approval of the Roman Procurator.

Pharisees

The Pharisees were far more influential among the people than the Sadducees. They were the progessive party of Judaism. For them religious life centred round the study and keeping of the Law of Moses. Their heritage can be traced back to the time of the destruction of the Temple in 586 BC, when the Jews were taken captive into exile by the Babylonians. All that the loyal Jew in exile had left to keep the faith alive was a strict keeping of the Law of Moses, contained in the Pentateuch. (The Pentateuch or the Torah is the Law of Moses found in the first five books of the Old Testament.)

In the second century BC, when Judah was occupied by the Greeks, the Pharisees were the ones who refused all Greek influences. They became known as the 'separated ones' (this is what the name Pharisee means) because of their refusal to compromise. Their aim was to keep alive the traditional Jewish faith.

WHAT THE PHARISEES BELIEVED

- The Pharisees wished to protect the Law and make it fit every need of daily life.
- They strictly kept the Oral Law, which was developed by the Scribes, to interpret the Law of Moses.
- In their desire to keep the Law, they surrounded it with:

    (a) a great many minute regulations;
    (b) volumes of explanations;

(c) all sort of complicated additions.
- This 'oral law' was equally as binding as the written Law of Moses. It was later written down in two books called the *Mishnah* and the *Talmud*.
- The Pharisees looked forward to the coming of the Messiah.
- The Pharisees believed in a form of the resurrection at the last day (the Day of Judgment).

Sadducees

The Sadducees claimed direct descent from Zadok who was the High Priest at the time of King Solomon (1 Kings 2:35). The Sadducees were priests. They were the upper class in Jewish society, living in ease and comfort. They had control of the Temple worship, sacrifices and finances. They were very conservative in their political outlook and wanted things to remain exactly as they were under the Romans. They were content, therefore, to work in co-operation with the Romans.

WHAT THE SADDUCEES BELIEVED

The beliefs of the Sadducees differed from other religious parties.

- They did not believe in the coming of the Messiah, especially the popular idea of the Messiah who would free the people from the Romans. This would lead to conflict with Rome and this must be avoided at all costs.
- Their only rule of religious, moral and social life was the *Law of Moses* as found in the first five books of the Old Testament (called the *Pentateuch* or the *Torah*). They took the Commandments of Moses literally.
- They laid little emphasis on the message of the prophets.
- They refused to be bound by the *'Oral Law'*, which explained the written Law of Moses (see Scribes and Pharisees).
- They did not believe in any form of resurrection.

Scribes

The Scribes belonged mainly, though not exclusively, to the party of the Pharisees. They were lawyers and sometimes are referred to as such in the Gospel.

The Scribes first appeared in the reign of Solomon. They became important in a world where few could write. Originally they were responsible for making accurate copies of the scriptures and for guarding the text against any errors. Slowly they became the legal authorities on the religious law, adding comments and interpretations of their own.

If parents wished their son to become a Scribe they took him to Jerusalem at the age of thirteen and enrolled him in one of the Rabbinical schools. His period of study lasted to the age of thirty when he became a Doctor of the Law.

The Temple

The Temple was central to Jewish belief. It symbolised the presence of God among the people.

The idea of the Temple went back to the time of Moses when God commanded a tabernacle (i.e. a tent) to be built in which to keep the Ark of the Covenant. The Ark was a portable shrine which accompanied the Israelites in their wanderings in the Sinai desert (Exodus 25 and 26).

The first Temple dates from the reign of King Solomon, c.970–930 BC, and was built in Jerusalem. It was the centre of the religion. Only there could sacrificial worship take place (1 Kings 6).

This Temple was destroyed in 586 BC by the Babylonians. In 520 BC, on their return from exile, the Jews rebuilt the Temple.

A new and more splendid Temple was begun by Herod the Great in 20 BC. This was the Temple that Jesus knew, although it was not completed until after his death in 64 AD. Six years later, in 70 AD, this new Temple was destroyed by the Romans.

Herod's Temple was a magnificent building. It included the following features:

(a) **Court of the Gentiles**. This was a public place used as a market where traders sold the birds and animals used for sacrifices.

In this court could be found the money changers who changed the 'unclean' currencies such as Roman money into the sacred Temple money for the payment of Temple collections.

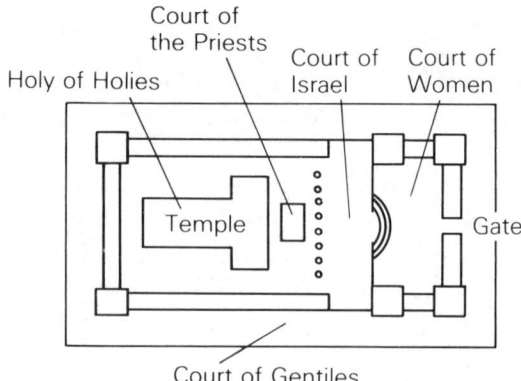

(b) **Court of Israel**. Only Jewish males were allowed in this court. Gentiles were forbidden to enter. There was a separate court for women. Again Gentiles were not allowed to enter.

(c) **Court of the Priests.** This was the most exclusive court. Only the priests were allowed to enter. In this area was the altar of sacrifice on which the birds and animals were killed.

(d) **Holy of Holies.** The Holy of Holies was the innermost shrine of the Temple. It was screened by a large veil or curtain. Behind it was the altar of incense.

The Holy of Holies was reserved for the presence of God. No one but the officiating priest was allowed to approach this most sacred place.

Temple Worship

The importance of the Temple worship, for the Jew of Jesus' day, can hardly be overestimated. The idea of sacrifice was central to this worship. There were three different types of sacrifice.

(a) **Morning and evening sacrifice**. Both took the form of the offering of incense; the sacrifice of a lamb without blemish; and the meal offering of flour and oil – all of which was accompanied by prayer and praise.

(b) **Private offerings – daily**. Each day individuals would ask for private sacrifices to be offered to God in thanksgiving or forgiveness for sins.

(c) **Feast days**. On feast days such as Passover, thousands of offerings were made.

All sacrifices were intended as a means of obtaining the forgiveness of God. The climax of the sacrificial year was the Day of Atonement when the High Priest entered the Holy of Holies and offered the blood of sacrifice as atonement for all the sins of Israel.

Once a year, at the Feast of Passover, vast numbers of Jewish pilgrims came to Jerusalem from all over to celebrate the Exodus. At this time the Temple resembled a huge slaughterhouse as thousands of lambs were sacrificed and handed to the people for the celebration of the Passover meal that night.

Temple worship ceased after the destruction of the Temple in 70 AD. All that remains of Herod the Great's Temple is a course of huge stones where the Jews meet daily for prayer. This is called the Western Wall, popularly called the Wailing Wall because Jews bewail the destruction of the Temple there.

The Synagogue

There was only one Temple but there was a synagogue in every Jewish community. The word 'synagogue' is a Greek word meaning 'assembly' or 'meeting' and represents the gathering of a congregation. As with the word 'church', the synagogue came to stand for the building as well as the people meeting there.

The origin of the synagogue goes back to the Babylonian period. The Jews were in exile after 586 BC and found themselves cut off from the temple. They evolved a form of worship which required neither priest, Temple nor sacrifice. They gathered together to read the scriptures and to pray. They found this to be so worthwhile that, on their return from exile, synagogue worship continued and became a major influence in religious life.

The synagogue was administered by a council of 'elders' who appointed a 'ruler' whose duty it was to prepare for the daily services and provide some general supervision. There were three services each day, at 9.00 a.m., 12.00 noon and 3.00 p.m.

Synagogue worship is very important to the Jews. Since the destruction of the Temple in 70 AD, it has been the synagogue that has kept the Jewish faith alive throughout the centuries even to the present day.

Understanding the Synoptic Gospels

The Formation of Gospel Tradition

In the earliest years of the Christian Church there was little need for a written record of the events of Jesus' life, death and resurrection. They had been observed by the disciples and passed on by word of mouth. That was sufficient because the early Christians expected

Jesus to return immediately and set up the reign of God on earth. (This event is called the *parousia*.)

As Christianity spread through the Roman Empire, so the stories of Jesus also spread. It is natural that some of these stories were developed and adapted to make the message of the Gospel relevant to people of differing backgrounds to the Jews.

In 66 AD the Jews rebelled against their Roman overlords in Palestine. This resulted in Jerusalem being destroyed in 70 AD. James, the leader of the Jerusalem Church, was killed at this time. At about the same time, far away in Rome, Christians were being persecuted by the Emperor Nero. Thousands of Christians lost their lives. Amongst them, according to tradition, were St Peter and St Paul.

Jesus had not returned and the first generation Christians were beginning to die. Now the 'Gospel', the good news about Jesus, had to be preserved. The traditions about Jesus were collected and formed into books by the Evangelists. Of the many Gospels written, the Church, later on, chose four as being the ones that contained 'the faith'. These four were the ones named Matthew, Mark, Luke and John.

Oral Tradition

After the death and resurrection of Jesus, the stories about his life were passed on by word of mouth for some thirty years before the first Gospel was written. This is called the period of the 'oral tradition'.

The study of the oral tradition is called *form criticism*. Form criticism examines the way in which the traditions of Jesus were preserved and handed on in the time before the writing of the Gospels.

The form critics claim:

- The stories about Jesus can be categorised into four main 'forms'. These can be seen clearly in the Gospel narrative.
- The four forms are:
  (a) pronouncement stories (called 'paradigms'). These are stories that lead to an important statement by Jesus. For example, the story of Jesus having dinner at Levi's house leads to Jesus telling the Pharisees, 'I did not come to call the virtuous but sinners' (Mark 2:17);
  (b) miracle stories (all following a set pattern);
  (c) biographical sketches. These are stories that provide more

    detail about a specific person (see Luke 19:1–10); and
    (d) parables.
- The reason for the preserving and passing on of the traditions in this way was that they were used primarily by the early Church in its teaching of the community.
- The form critics claim that some development of the stories took place in the passing down of these traditions.
- Each story was separate and passed on in isolation with the possible exception of the story of the Passion.
- The context of each story in the Gospel was in the hands of the author himself.

When each Evangelist recorded the stories about Jesus he did so for a particular purpose. He did not write a biography. He wrote with a particular audience in mind and therefore emphasised the points of interest most suited to that audience. The study of the author's influence on the oral tradition is called *redaction criticism*.

The redaction critics claim:

- It is important to realise that the Gospel writers were not writing history as we understand it.
- They were not interested in the question 'What really happened?' They took for granted the historical events of Jesus: his birth, life, death and resurrection. The question they sought to answer was much more important. They asked continually, 'What does this mean for us?'

    For example they would ask 'What does it mean for Jesus to die on the cross?' rather than 'What happened when Jesus was crucified?'
- It is inevitable that the Evangelist made changes to the traditions in his desire to say what the events of Jesus' life meant for his readers.

The Relationship Between the Synoptic Gospels

The first three Gospels, Matthew, Mark and Luke, if placed side by side, are seen, at one and the same time, to be both similar and dissimilar. This is known as the *synoptic problem*. The word 'synoptic' is a combination of two Greek words:

syn = together
opsis = view or sight

Before a solution to this problem can be offered, the similarities and differences must be examined.

Similarities

Content

The three Gospels record the same basic outline of the words and deeds of Jesus. Almost the whole of Mark's Gospel is found in Matthew and Luke taken together.

(a) Mark has only some thirty verses which are not repeated in one or both of the other two Gospels.

(b) About 95 per cent of Mark is contained in Matthew and 65 per cent of Mark is contained in Luke.

(c) In addition Matthew and Luke have material in common not found in Mark. There are 171 verses of Matthew that are closely paralleled by 151 verses in Luke; and 90 verses of Matthew are loosely paralleled by 94 in Luke.

(d) There is also material which is found only in Matthew (282 verses) and in Luke (490 verses).

Arrangement

The three Gospels cover the same course of the life and work of Jesus.

	Matthew	**Mark**	**Luke**
John the Baptist and the baptism of Jesus	3:1–4:11	1:1–13	3:1–4:13
Galilean ministry and journeys in the north to Gentile territory	4:12–18:35	1:14–9:50	4:14–9:50
Journey to Jerusalem	19:1–20:34	10:1–52	9:51–18:43
Passion and Resurrection	21:1–28:20	11:1–16:8	19:1–24:53

Language

A comparison of the three Gospels shows not only that they have a great deal in common but also that, in many cases, the wording of individual stories is either identical or very similar (for example, compare Mark 2:3–12; Matt. 9:2–8; Luke 5:18–26).

Perhaps it is not all that surprising to find the same stories in three books about the same person. What is surprising, however, is that such stories are told using the same, or very nearly the same, language. This must mean that there is a written connection between the three.

The question is, who wrote his Gospel first?

There is also close similarity in language in certain stories found only in Matthew and Luke (for example, compare Matt. 3:7–10; Luke 3:7–9).

Differences

Content
There are differences between the three accounts. Some events or stories are recorded by only two of the Evangelists (for example, the healing of the centurion's servant (Matt. 8:5–13; Luke 7:1–10)).

Some stories are recorded only by one of the Evangelists (for example, the Parable of the Good Samaritan (Luke 10:29–37)).

Even in some cases where two or three of the Evangelists record the same event, their accounts differ considerably (for example, the resurrection narratives).

Arrangement
There are differences in arrangement. Each writer does not follow exactly the same order in the arrangement of his material. For example, Luke has only one story outside of Galilee in the first section of his Gospel (the healing of Legion (Luke 8:26–39), whereas Matthew and Mark record a more extensive ministry in Gentile country (Matt. 14:22–16:4; Mark 6:45–8:13).

Language
It must be noted that, while there is great similarity of language in many passages recorded in all three Gospels, there are differences. The accounts are not exactly the same.

Solutions

1 Mark is the Earliest Gospel and is used as a Source by the Other Two

There is widespread agreement that Mark was the first Gospel to be completed and that he became a prime source of both Matthew and Luke. There are four main reasons for this viewpoint:

(a) When a study is made of passages that appear in all three Gospels, there are very few occasions when Matthew and Luke agree on wording against Mark. Normally, when the language is different, one of them agrees with Mark.

(b) The order of events in Mark forms the basis of the other two Gospels. Sometimes Matthew or Luke depart from Mark's order of events but never at the same time together and they always return to it.

(c) Both Matthew and Luke improve the poor style of Mark's Gospel.

(d) Mark's accounts of stories are the longest. It is more likely that the accounts in Matthew and Luke are shortened versions of Mark than that Mark has expanded one of theirs. Therefore, many scholars conclude that Mark is a source of Matthew and Luke.

2 Matthew and Luke use Another Source

There are some 250 verses which are found in both Matthew and Luke but not in Mark. Again the wording of the stories is either identical or very similar (for example, compare Matthew 3:7–10; Luke 3:7–9). This close similarity indicates a second written source. It is not known what this source was. The letter 'Q' is used to represent the source (the first letter of the German word *Quelle*, meaning 'source').

'Q' is a collection of some of the teachings of Jesus (for example, the temptations (Luke 4:1–13; Matt. 4:1–11) and the centurion's servant (Luke 7:1–10; Matt. 8:5–13)).

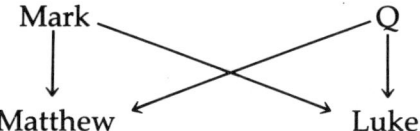

3 Matthew's Own Source

In addition to material from Mark and 'Q', Matthew has material peculiar to himself. This material is normally referred to as 'M'. It contains his account of the birth and resurrection of Jesus, plus a collection of various sayings and parables.

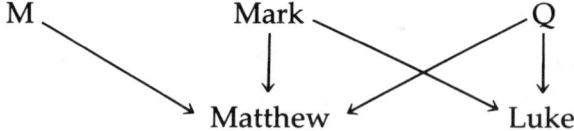

4 Luke's Own Source

There is also a lot of material that is found only in Luke's Gospel. This material is generally referred to as 'L'. It is doubtful if this existed in a written form and it could well have been an oral source which Luke knew of and used. 'L' is a source which contains miracles, parables and certain pieces of narrative concerning, for example, the Last Supper, and the death and resurrection of Jesus.

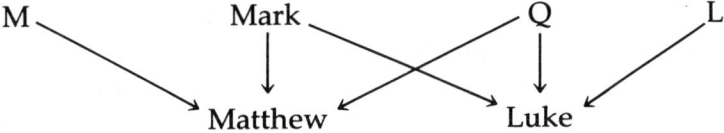

5 The Birth Stories of Luke

Some scholars think that the infancy stories in Luke's Gospel come from a separate source. Certainly their atmosphere is different from the rest of the Gospel. They seem to have their origin in Judaism far more than the rest of the book. This source can be called 'I'.

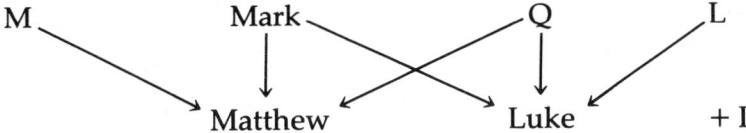

The Authorship and Date of the Synoptic Gospels

Mark

Who was Mark?

The New Testament mentions a John Mark quite a lot. If this is the same person as the author of the Gospel then it is possible to build up a picture of him.

(a) He lived in Jerusalem. There is a story in the Acts of the Apostles which describes how Peter, after he had escaped from prison, went to the house of Mary, the mother of John Mark (Acts 12:12).

(b) His names – John, a Jewish name, and Mark, a Latin name – suggest that he was a Greek-speaking Jew. They were called Hellenists.

(c) John Mark was not an apostle, yet he seems to have been closely involved with three of the principal characters of the early Church:

Peter sends greetings from Rome from himself and Mark, whom he calls 'my son' (1 Peter 5:13);

Barnabas was Mark's cousin and he stood by him when there was a dispute with Paul (Acts 15:36–40);

Paul was helped by Mark during the time when he was captive in Rome (Colossians 4:10; 2 Timothy 4:11).

These connections cannot be proved. Mark, after all, was one of the most common names in the Roman Empire.

(d) None of the Gospels contains the name of the author in the text. The titles were added later by the Church. It is quite likely, however, that there is a reference to the author in the young man who escaped and ran away naked (14:51) at the arrest of Jesus. This seems the only explanation of this verse that makes any sense.

(e) All the early evidence of the Church is unanimous in saying that Mark is the author of the Gospel and that he was closely connected with Peter. Bishop Eusebius (c.260–340) quotes Papias, a Bishop in Asia Minor in about 140 AD, who in turn quotes John the Elder who says: '... Mark, having become the interpreter of Peter, wrote down accurately, though not in order, all that he remembered of the things said and done by the Lord ...' There is also the quotation from Irenaeus (one of the early Church Fathers, 140–202 AD) who had been in Rome. Writing a hundred years before Eusebius, he states that, after the deaths of Peter and Paul, in the course of the persecutions in Rome: 'Mark the disciple and interpreter of Peter also handed down to us in writing the things preached by Peter.'

(f) It would be a mistake, however, to think that the Markan Gospel of the New Testament is merely the notes of, or the preaching of, Peter. Whatever information Mark received from Peter, it is certain that, by the time he wrote his finished Gospel, development and adaptation of much of the material had taken place. Indeed, many of the stories were already in existence in an oral form.

The Date of Mark's Gospel

If the Gospel was written by the John Mark who is mentioned in the Acts of the Apostles, then it must have been written in the first generation of the Christian Church, between 35 and 75 AD.

Peter was probably martyred in Rome during the persecutions of Nero in 64–5 AD. An early prologue attached to Mark's Gospel says that Mark wrote after the death of Peter in Italy. Irenaeus says that Mark wrote after the deaths of Peter and Paul, while Clement of Alexandria stated that the book was written while Peter was still preaching in Rome. Therefore, the date of the Gospel is likely to have been in the decade 60–70 AD.

The Gospel contains a large amount of material concerned with the theme of suffering and persecution. It is reasonable to assume, therefore, that it was written during or immediately after the persecutions in Rome. This would date the book around 65–70 AD.

Most of the early Christian authorities claim the place of writing was Rome, although St Jerome, writing much later, says the Gospel was written in Alexandria. This seems unlikely in view of the overwhelming claim of the early authorities that the Gospel was written in Rome.

Matthew

For a long time it was thought that this Gospel was written by Matthew the Apostle. There are, however, good reasons for questioning this assumption.

(a) The basis of the book seems to be Mark's Gospel; a Gospel not written by an eyewitness. It is strange that, if Matthew the Apostle was the author, he would use someone else's work as his own basic source. This is true especially of the story of his own call to be a disciple, which he has copied from Mark.

(b) The way Matthew treats the Markan source does not suggest that he knew more about the events concerned because he was an Apostle. He makes the Markan account less vivid.

(c) The author is not aware of the historical and religious conditions in Palestine at the time of Jesus. For example, he makes a Greek woman use a Jewish Messianic title (Matt. 15:21). He refers throughout his Gospel to the Pharisees and Sadducees, two very different groups, as though they were very close.

(d) Matthew includes stories which are the least reliable from the point of view of history. His birth stories contradict those of Luke; his additions to the Passion stories are all heightened and are looked upon with suspicion as to their historicity. They are hardly the writings of an eyewitness (see, for example, the dream of Pilate's wife, Pilate's hand-washing, the death of Judas, the guard at the tomb, the earthquake, and the resurrection of the saints).

Whereas it is impossible to identify the author of this Gospel, it is possible to be sure of one thing about him. He was a Jewish Christian, writing for Jewish Christians (see the characteristics of the Gospel).

The Date of Matthew's Gospel

The Gospel must have been written after 65–70 AD if Mark is one of his sources.

Many scholars believe the Gospel was written after 70 AD.

- They claim that the Gospel shows a knowledge of the destruction of Jerusalem 70 AD (Matt. 22:7).
- Little distinction is made between the Jewish religious parties.

This may be because the Sadducees, as a party, ceased to exist after the destruction of the Temple in 70 AD.
- There is great emphasis on the Church in this Gospel and time must be allowed for such a development of the Church to have taken place (especially Matt. 18:15–17).
- Baptism in the name of the Father and of the Son and of the Holy Spirit (Matt. 28:19) suggests a later date as the evidence from the Acts of the Apostles suggests that baptism in the earliest days of the Church was in the name of Jesus only (Acts 2:38).

Matthew's Gospel is usually dated 80–5 AD. It is not known where the Gospel was written but it must have been written for a Jewish Christian community. Antioch in Syria has been suggested as a likely place.

Luke

(a) All historical evidence says that the Gospel was written by someone called Luke.

(b) One example of this early evidence can be found in the Muratorian Canon. (This is the earliest copy of the *Canon of Scripture*: the books of the Bible chosen to represent the faith of the Church.) It contains this statement:

'The third Gospel according to Luke. After the Ascension of Christ, Luke, whom Paul had taken with him as an expert in the way (teaching), wrote under his own name and according to his own understanding. He had not, of course, seen the Lord in the flesh, and therefore, he begins to tell the story from the birth of John on.'

(c) Luke's superb Greek style and his emphasis on universalism lead many people to believe that he was of Gentile origin with Greek as his native language. He was, however, very knowledgeable in Jewish teaching and scripture.

(d) Luke was not an eye-witness, otherwise he would not have used Mark as a source. He says in the prologue to the Gospel that he was not a witness to the events themselves (1:1–4).

(e) Some scholars claim that Luke was a doctor. This is based on the comment by Paul in his letter to the Colossians where he writes, 'Greetings to you from our dear friend Luke, the doctor' (Colossians 4:14).

(f) Whoever the author was, he wrote two books. The Acts of the Apostles is written in the same hand. It may be that the two books were originally one manuscript.

(g) The author seems to have been a companion and friend of St Paul. A certain Luke is mentioned in his letters (2 Timothy 4:11; Philemon 24; Colossians 4:14).

(h) In the Acts of the Apostles there are three sections known as the 'we-passages'. These are passages where the author suddenly starts talking about what 'we did'. In the rest of the book he talks about what 'they did'. The obvious conclusion is that the writer himself was present on these occasions and has written some form of daily record or diary.

Two conclusions have been drawn from this evidence:

1. Luke, companion of Paul, wrote them both.
2. Luke wrote only the diary when he was with Paul on his journeys and someone else wrote the books. The name Luke was given to the books.

The Date of Luke's Gospel

There are two possible dates:

An early date

The Acts of the Apostles ends with the imprisonment of St Paul in Rome awaiting trial. According to tradition, Paul was executed in the persecutions of Christians in Rome around 65 AD. This fact is not found in the Acts of the Apostles even though it would be a logical conclusion to the book. Could Luke have finished his Gospel before Paul's death? It is doubtful if this could be the case if he used Mark as his main source as that Gospel was not written until about 65 AD.

Some people seem to think that Luke wrote an early draft of his Gospel containing only the material from 'Q' and 'L' (this is called *Proto-Luke*). If this were so, then certainly this material could be as early as 60–5 AD.

A later date

If Mark is the main source of the Gospel then the date of Luke must be later than his. It must be after 65–70 AD. Luke's Gospel also contains references to the fall of Jerusalem which took place in 70 AD (Luke 21:20). So the completed Gospel is dated at around 75–80 AD.

The Characteristics of the Synoptic Gospels

Mark

(a) The Gospel was written in primitive Greek. It has been

suggested that Greek was not the native language of the author but that he wrote in the universal language of the day which was Greek, while thinking in his own language which was probably Aramaic.

(b) There are certain details in the Gospel which make scholars think that there is an authentic eye-witness standing behind the Gospel story in some of the accounts. In view of the evidence of the early Fathers of the Christian Church, this was most probably Peter. There is, for example, a mention of a 'cushion' in the calming of the storm (Mark 4:38) and of 'green grass' in the feeding of the 5000 (Mark 6:39).

(c) The Gospel is not written for Jewish readers. Mark explains Jewish customs and Aramaic expressions throughout the book. For example, he translates the word 'Golgotha' (Mark 15:22) and 'Eli, Eli, lema sabachthani' (Mark 15:34).

(d) The major theme of the Gospel is *suffering*. It is not surprising that this is so considering the background in Rome against which the Gospel is written. Jesus is the Messiah who must suffer and die in order to rise from the dead and return to establish God's kingdom on earth. Suffering is so prominent a part of the Gospel that it has been described as a Passion story with an introduction. The rumblings of death appear as early as Mark 3:6 after the stories of conflict with the religious authorities. From chapter 8 onwards the theme of suffering is the major preoccupation of the book. The final week of Jesus occupies one-third of the Gospel.

Matthew

(a) **Jewish Christianity**. Matthew writes for Jewish Christians and in so doing displays Jewish characteristics in his book. The most obvious of these is that he frequently quotes the Old Testament. He uses a set formula: 'this was to fulfil the words spoken through the prophet' (Matt. 2:17, 23; 4:12–16; 12:15–21; 13:34–35; 21:2–7).

(b) **Eschatology and parousia**. Matthew shows a great interest in *eschatology* (the teaching about the end of the world) and *parousia* (the teaching about the second coming of Jesus) (Matt. 16:28). This is most obvious in the parables coming from Matthew's own source (the parable of the wheat and tares (Matt. 13:24–30, 37–40), the parable of the dragnet (Matt. 13:47–50), the parable of the ten bridesmaids (Matt. 25:1–13), and the final judgment (Matt. 25:31–46).

(c) **Emphasis on the miraculous**. Matthew tends to heighten the miraculous. Sometimes he does this by changing his sources. For example, Legion becomes two madmen (Matt. 8:28); blind

Bartimaeus becomes two blind men (Matt. 20:29). Sometimes Matthew introduces new material which is highly miraculous in its content. For example, there is an earthquake and opening of the tombs at the crucifixion (Matt. 27:51–53).

(d) **Church**. Matthew places a great emphasis on the Church. This is the only Gospel where Jesus proclaims Peter as the rock on which the Church is to be built (Matt. 16:18). In fact this is the only Gospel to use the word 'Church' (Matt. 16:18; 18:17) and includes material from the experience of the early Church (Matt. 18).

Some scholars, however, see Matthew's interest in the Church as going beyond the mere mention of the word. In Matthew the disciples stand for the Church, as does the phrase 'the kingdom of heaven'.

Finally, the whole of the Gospel leads to the commission of the Church, to go out and baptise, to teach, and to pass on the new law of Christianity (Matt. 28:18–20).

Luke

(a) By the time Luke wrote his Gospel the Romans had begun to persecute Christians. Luke's overall purpose is to try to show that the growing movement of Christianity is in no way dangerous to the state of Rome. It is, therefore, not surprising to find in Luke that it is the Jews who are blamed for the death of Jesus. The Roman authorities are treated with a respect which is almost excusing them from any responsibility.

(b) It must not be forgotten that Luke is the author of two books in the New Testament: the Gospel and the Acts of the Apostles. In the Acts he shows how Christianity slowly spread, from the beginning on the day of Pentecost, into the Roman Empire. In the Gospel, Luke shows how Jesus moves towards Jerusalem in order for all this to take place through the death and resurrection of Jesus.

Luke's purpose can be expressed in a simple diagram.

Certain other characteristics in the Gospel are used to support this main purpose of Luke.

(c) **Luke the historian**. Even though Luke is not trying to answer the question, 'What happened?', he is at pains to set his account in a historical setting. He tries to fix dates at the key time of Jesus' birth and beginning of his ministry (Luke 2:1; 3:1).

(d) **Universalism**. One major characteristic of the Gospel is its universalism. The Gospel is for all mankind, not just for the Jews (Luke 2:14, 32; 3:6; 4:16–30; 7:9; 9:52; 10:30–35; 17:12; 24:47).

(e) **Sympathy for the poor and sinners**. The Gospel shows Jesus as a friend of outcasts, sinners and the poor (Luke 7:37; 14:15ff.; 15:1ff.; 19:1–10).

(f) **The importance given to women**. In New Testament times women were largely uneducated, and had no legal rights and no place in public life. In contrast to this, women play an important role in the Gospel. In the infancy narratives the role played by Mary and Elizabeth is a major one (Luke 1:5–80; 2:1–52). In addition Luke records other stories involving women to a far greater extent than the other Gospels (Luke 7:11ff., 37ff.; 8:1–2; 10:38–42; 21:1–4; 23:50–24:11).

(g) **The emphasis on prayer**. Each of the Gospels mentions how Jesus went away into the hills to pray. Luke, however, has teaching on the subject of prayer that is not found in the other Gospels (Luke 11:5–9; 18:1–8, 9–14). He also includes examples of early Christian prayers (called *canticles*) in his infancy narratives (Luke 1:46ff., 67ff.; 2:14, 29ff.).

(h) **The Gospel of the Holy Spirit**. Luke has been called the *Gospel of the Holy Spirit*. His first two chapters are a record of the creative action of the Spirit (Luke 1:15, 35, 41, 67; 2:25–36). Jesus is guided by the Spirit (Luke 3:22; 4:1, 18; 10:21). At the moment of death Jesus hands back the Spirit to God (Luke 23:46). The Holy Spirit is promised to the disciples after the resurrection (Luke 24:49).

CHAPTER

2 The Birth Stories of Jesus

The purpose of this chapter is to look at the infancy stories about Jesus as recorded by both Matthew and Luke. This can be done by examining:

- The differences between Matthew's and Luke's accounts
- The text of the birth stories
    1. The announcement of the birth of Jesus (Matt. 1:18–25; Luke 1:26–38)
    2. The birth of Jesus according to Matthew (Matt. 2:1–23)
    3. The birth of Jesus according to Luke (Luke 2:1–20)
    4. The circumcision and presentation of Jesus (Luke 2:21–40)
    5. The boy Jesus in the Temple (Luke 2:41–52)

The Differences Between Matthew's and Luke's Accounts

Matthew and Luke are the only Gospels to record the birth of Jesus. The problem is that they do not agree on the facts surrounding this event. The only agreement between them is that the birth of Jesus took place in the reign of Herod the Great, in the town of Bethlehem, and that Mary and Joseph were the names of his parents. After this they have little in common. Rather the rest is contradictory, as can be seen from the following table.

	Matthew	Luke
1		Mary lives in Nazareth. She receives a visit from the Angel Gabriel who announces that she will conceive and bear a child (Luke 1:26–33).
2	Joseph's doubts about Mary's faithfulness are dispelled by the Angel of the Lord, place unknown (Matt. 1:18–25).	
3		Mary and Joseph travel to Bethlehem as a result of a census (Luke 2:1–5).
4	Mary is placed in Bethlehem from the start (Matt. 2:1).	
5	In the reign of Herod the Great (Matt. 2:1).	In the reign of Herod the Great (Luke 1:5).

	Matthew	Luke
6		Jesus is born in Bethlehem; placed in a manger. The angels appear to the shepherds in the fields, who then go to the town to see for themselves (Luke 2:6–20).
7	The Magi arrive at Jerusalem from the east (Matt. 2:1).	
8	They follow the star. After a consultation with Herod, they arrive at the house where the child is (Matt. 2:2–11a).	
9	They offer gifts of gold, frankincense and myrrh (Matt 2:11b).	
10	They do not return to Herod (Matt. 2:12).	
11	Joseph and Mary flee with Jesus to Egypt, to escape Herod (Matt. 2:13–15).	
12		After the circumcision of Jesus and the purification of Mary, the family return to Nazareth (Luke 2:21–39).
13	The massacre of the innocents by Herod (Matt. 2:16–18).	
14	The family return from Egypt and settle, for the first time, in Nazareth, to escape Archelaus who had succeeded Herod (Matt. 2:19–23).	

At first, the differences between the two accounts may be disturbing, especially if the accounts are thought of as simple historical records of the birth of Jesus. It must be remembered, however, that the Gospel writers are not concerned simply with history but are also interested in what the event of the birth of Jesus means (see chapter 1).

The Text of the Birth Stories

The Announcement of the Birth of Jesus (Matt. 1:18–25; Luke 1:26–38)

Matthew

Matthew records the announcement of the birth of Jesus from Joseph's point of view.

Mary is engaged to be married to Joseph. Before the marriage she is discovered to be pregnant. Joseph, who is certain he is not the father of the child, decides to 'divorce' Mary quietly to avoid public scandal. It must be understood that engagement in those days was a very serious matter which involved a written contract of intent to marry and needed legal consent if the engagement was to be broken off.

Before Joseph can take any action, however, he is told in a dream, by the 'Angel of the Lord', that the child is to be born because God wishes it. Joseph accepts the message and marries Mary.

The message of the Angel of the Lord, in Matthew's Gospel, is very clear:

> ... she has conceived what is in her by the Holy Spirit (*Matt. 1:20*).

This verse is the clearest statement in the New Testament about the virginal conception of Jesus. Mary was to conceive a child without the ususal help of the male. The birth would be the result of the direct intervention of the creative power of the Holy Spirit.

The baby was to be named Jesus, which means 'God is salvation'. Matthew states from the outset that the purpose of this child will be to offer salvation from sin or, in other words, bring people back to God.

Having reached the high-water mark in his claim for the nature and purpose of the birth of Jesus, Matthew goes on to cause all sorts of problems for the modern reader. One of the characteristics of Matthew is his desire to prove Jesus as the fulfilment of Jewish hope and promise by quoting from the Old Testament. Unfortunately, his quotations are often taken out of context and are sometimes inaccurate. In this account of the announcement of the birth of Jesus to Joseph, Matthew quotes the prophet Isaiah (7:14).

> The virgin will conceive and give birth to a son and they will call him Immanuel (*Mark 1:23*).

Matthew goes on to translate 'Immanuel' as 'God-is-with-us' (Matt. 1:23).

This quotation poses two problems:

1 The quotation from Isaiah is not part of the Jewish scriptures normally associated with the expectation of the Messiah.
2 Matthew quotes from the Greek translation of the Old Testament (called the *Septuagint*). In this version the word used for 'virgin' is the Greek word *parthenos*, which means 'virgin' in the sexual sense of the word. Unfortunately this is a mis-translation of the original Hebrew of Isaiah. Isaiah used the Hebrew word *almah*, which simply means 'a young woman' and carries no sexual meaning whatsoever.

Even though Matthew's use of this text is invalid, there is no doubt that the verse became accepted by the Christian Church as evidence for the miraculous birth of Jesus.

Luke

Luke records the announcement of the birth of Jesus from Mary's point of view.

Luke writes that the Angel Gabriel was sent to a town called Nazareth, in Galilee, to a girl called Mary. Mary was engaged to be married to Joseph, who came from Bethlehem, the house of David, near Jerusalem in Judaea.

Mary was a virgin. Luke is most anxious to make this clear and he uses the Greek word *parthenos* twice in the opening sentence. *Parthenos*, as we have seen, means 'virgin' in the sexual sense of the word. This word is sometimes translated as 'girl' (Luke 1:26–38).

The opening words of the angel form the beginning of the prayer called the 'Hail Mary'. The words can be translated:

> Hail (Mary) full of grace, the Lord is with you (*Luke 1:28*).

The angel goes on to inform Mary that she is to have a child. All the Jewish hopes and thoughts of the Messiah are summed up in the words of the angel.

- The child will be called Jesus, a name meaning 'God is salvation'.
- He is described as 'great'. This adjective is normally reserved for God in the Old Testament.
- His title will be 'Son of the Most High'. This is an alternative for the title 'Son of God'.
- Like his ancestor, King David, he will rule over Israel but his reign will be for ever.

Mary obviously understands the message of the angel to mean that she will conceive a child immediately, for she points out that she is unmarried. The angel's answer is part of the foundation of the teaching about the virgin birth. Conception was to be brought about by the creative power of God, through the Holy Spirit. As a result of this, the child would be called 'Son of God'. The words indicate clearly the virginal conception of Jesus (Luke 1:34–35).

Mary accepted the message of the angel with complete trust and obedience. She is prepared to trust God and the story closes with the simplest words of acceptance:

> I am the Lord's servant; as you have spoken, so be it (*Luke 1:38*).

The Importance of the virgin birth for Christians today

Even though the phrase that Jesus was 'born of the Virgin Mary' is found in the creeds of the universal Christian Church, Christians are divided on the interpretation of this event. Some would consider the story to be historically important; others see its importance only in terms of the developing faith of the Church.

Those who take the former view claim:

- *It is important that the birth of Jesus was unique. They would say that this was the only fitting way for the Son of God to be born.*
- *Both Matthew and Luke have recorded the event in historical terms.*
- *The event was prophesied in the Old Testament.*
- *It cannot be proved that the virgin birth did not happen.*

Those taking the later view claim:

- *There is no knowledge of the idea of the virgin birth in the Church before the Gospels were written.*
- *The stories were constructed to 'fulfil' the Old Testament prophecies.*
- *The stories illustrate the Church's understanding of who Jesus was.*
- *It cannot be proved the virgin birth happened.*

The Birth of Jesus According to Matthew (Matt. 2:1–23)

The Visit of the Wise Men (Matt. 2:1–12)

Matthew does not actually record the birth of Jesus. He takes up the story after the birth in Bethlehem with the arrival of the wise men from the east. The purpose of this story of the wise men is to make clear that the kingdom of God is open to all people. Even at the birth of the Christ, representatives of the Gentile world appear to pay homage to the new-born infant king. They arrive, having followed the star, and present their gifts to the child.

COMMENT ON THE WISE MEN

- Matthew places his account of the wise men in a historical setting. Herod the Great served the Roman Empire as the king of Judaea from 37–4 BC.
- Even so, some scholars question how much Matthew is dealing with history in this story of the wise men. They believe that in this passage, as with the rest of the chapter,

> there is much that is symbolism, used by Matthew to say what the birth of Jesus means to him.
> - They quote parallel stories of astrologers reading in the stars the birth of great men. For example, a star is mentioned in the account of the birth of Alexander the Great. In the ancient world, the belief was that each person was represented by a star.
> - More importantly, they point out that, as well as the obvious Old Testament quotations used by Matthew, there are many other references to the Old Testament. For example:
>   (a) The star which guided the wise men could be a reference to a well-known Old Testament text:
>   'a star shall come forth out of Jacob,
>   a comet arise from Israel' (Numbers 24:17).
>   Any devout Jew would recognise this 'star from Jacob' as referring to David in a Messianic sense.
>   (b) The arrival of the wise men and the offering of their gifts are also reflected in the Old Testament:
>   '... the nations shall march towards your light
>   and their kings to your sunrise ...
>   all coming from Sheba
>   laden with gold and frankincense,
>   heralds of God's praise' (Isaiah 60:3, 6; see also Psalms 72:10).
> - The purpose of Matthew is to portray Jesus as the Messiah, and therefore he writes his account using Old Testament Messianic texts.

The Flight into Egypt and Massacre of the Innocents (Matt. 2:13–18)

Luke states that, after the circumcision of Jesus and the purification of Mary, they returned to Nazareth (Luke 2:21–39).

Matthew is in complete disagreement. He reintroduces the Angel of the Lord, who appears again in Joseph's dreams with a message of danger. Joseph is instructed to escape to Egypt where they will be safe from Herod, who intends to kill all boys who are two years old and under, in an attempt to be rid of this new so-called king.

Again, many scholars see the sole reason for Matthew placing

Jesus in Egypt as that he is then able to show Jesus as the fulfilment of another Old Testament statement found in the book of the prophet Hosea: I called my son out of Egypt (Hosea 11:1). Hosea's words have nothing whatever to do with the birth of the Messiah. It is the opening verse of a chapter which recalls the time when God, through Moses, called the children of Isreal out of Egypt.

It seems impossible that Matthew and his readers were not aware of the original meaning of these words. It is much more likely that Matthew has purposely used a verse that would point towards Jesus as the new Moses who would, once again, lead his people from slavery to freedom. This time the slavery was that of sin, and the freedom that of being brought back to God.

This suggestion certainly seems to make sense when put into the context of the story of the massacre of the innocents. The murder of the baby boys by Herod is very similar to the story of Moses: he also escaped the killing of the Israelites' baby sons by Pharaoh (Exodus 1:15–2:10).

The history of the massacre by Herod the Great is doubtful. There is no mention of such an event in any other historical literature of this time.

Matthew concludes this section with a reference, again out of context, from the prophet Jeremiah. The quotation has nothing to do with the coming of the Messiah but refers to the destruction of the northern kingdom of Israel by Assyria in 721 BC. Matthew adapts the quotation as a useful conclusion to this story of the massacre of the innocents as Rachel, the mother of Benjamin and wife of Jacob, was buried near Jerusalem.

From Egypt to Nazareth (Matt. 2:19–23)

Matthew has to place Jesus in the right location, where he grew up, which is Nazareth in Galilee and not Egypt. He does this by introducing, once more, the Angel of the Lord. The message of the angel is simple: return to Israel because Herod is dead. Once more Joseph is obedient and sets out for his own country. On the way he discovers that Archelaus, Herod's son, is now ruler of Judaea. Archelaus was a cruel man and Joseph has no wish to live under his rule. The family therefore travels north to the territory of Galilee and settles, for the first time, in Nazareth.

Matthew claims all this took place to fulfil the words of the prophet:

He shall be called a Nazarene (*Matt. 2:23*).

On this note Matthew ends his account of the birth of Jesus. He has given a vivid portrayal of Jesus as the Messiah; the new Moses; the representative of God. On the one hand, this new-born child received the homage of Gentile kings. On the other hand, he received, even in infancy, the opposition that was to be repeated throughout his life, ending with crucifixion.

COMMENT ON MATTHEW 2:23

- The words 'He shall be called a Nazarene' are not an authentic verse. They do not appear anywhere in the Old Testament.
- It is impossible that Matthew was mistaken or that he simply made up the verse as a climax to his birth story hoping that his readers would not notice.
- Some scholars believe that Matthew is making a play on words and that the original word was *Nezer*. There are no written vowel letters in Hebrew and so the words *Nazara* (as it was originally) and *Nezer* would appear as the same word, simply 'N Z R'.
- The word *Nezer* means 'branch'. It could be that Matthew is referring to the greatest text to be found in the Old Testament concerning the coming of the Messiah:
'Then a shoot shall grow from the stock of Jesse,
and a branch shall spring from his roots.
The spirit of the Lord shall rest upon him,
a spirit of wisdom and understanding,
a spirit of counsel and power,
a spirit of knowledge and the fear of the Lord' (Isaiah 11:1).

The Birth of Jesus According to Luke (Luke 2:1–20)

Luke begins his account of the birth of Jesus by trying to set it in the context of world history. In so doing he creates a problem that has not yet been solved. Luke claims that Caesar Augustus ordered a census to be taken but there is no record of a census happening at that time.

> *COMMENT ON THE DATE OF THE BIRTH OF JESUS*
> - It is possible to arrive at a probable date for the birth of Jesus.
> - Caesar Augustus rules from 30 BC to 14 AD. He ordered a census throughout the Roman world. This gives us the broad dates within which Jesus was born.
> - It is known from Egyptian history that, from 20 AD, a census of householders was taken every fourteen years.
> - It is also known that a similar census took place in Syria in 6 AD. Palestine fell within the area covered by the Syrian census.
> - If, therefore, the fourteen-year rule applied to Syria as well as Egypt, then there may have been an earlier census in 8 BC, a date that is not too early for the birth of Jesus.
> - Luke claims that Quirinius was Governor of Syria. Josephus, the Jewish historian, states that Quirinius carried out the Syrian census in 6 AD. This date is too late for the birth of Jesus as it is well known that Jesus was born in the reign of Herod the Great, who died in 4 BC. Luke is wrong, therefore, in saying that the census carried out at the birth of Jesus was taken in the time of Quirinius.
> - Between 10 and 7 BC, however, Quirinius was known to be on military service in the Syrian area, and so there is the possibility of him being involved in a previous census even though he was not the Governor at the time.
> - In spite of all this, the actual year of the birth of Jesus remains unknown, although it was probably between 8 and 6 BC, bearing in mind the arguments above.

Luke states that everyone had to go to their home town to be registered. This was certainly possible. Such journeys are known to have happened. Joseph and Mary went to Bethlehem, the royal city of David, because Joseph belonged to that family.

Mary gave birth to Jesus in a Bethlehem outhouse, using a manger as a crib, because there was no room in the local inns.

At the moment of birth Luke says the Angel of the Lord appeared to some shepherds, announcing the message of the birth. After the announcement, the angel was joined by

> a great company of the heavenly host, singing the praises of God (*Luke 2:13*).

The shepherds hurried to the city to see for themselves. They spread the joyful news throughout the whole neighbourhood, while Mary treasured up all these things and pondered over them (*Luke 2:19*).

> *COMMENT ON THE BIRTH OF JESUS AS RECORDED BY LUKE*
>
> - At first sight, Luke, far more than Matthew, seems to be concerned to set the events of Jesus' birth in a historical setting. Yet the question must be asked as to how much Luke is writing an historical record, and how much, he, like Matthew, is more concerned with the importance of this new-born baby.
> - Though not as obvious as Matthew, Luke also writes his story with Old Testament overtones, combining them with basic historical facts.
> - The whole story of Jesus' birth seems to be an expansion of an Old Testament prophecy found in Micah:
> 'But you, Bethlehem . . .
> small as you are to be among Judah's clans,
> out of you shall come forth a governor for Israel,
> one whose roots are far back in the past, in days gone by.
> Therefore, only so long as a woman is in labour
> shall he give up Israel;
> and then those that survive of his race
> shall rejoin their brethren.
> He shall appear and be their shepherd
> in the strength of the Lord,
> in the majesty of the name of the Lord his God.
> And they shall continue, for now his greatness shall reach
> to the ends of the earth:
> and he shall be a man of peace' (Micah 5:2–5).
> - The message of Jesus' birth is given to the shepherds. It is traditional to see the shepherds as the poor, complementary to the wise men of Matthew's Gospel. It is certainly in keeping with Luke's attitude to the poor to present the news of the birth to the poor first of all. It should be noted, however, that the symbolism does not stop at this point. There is a further meaning to be discovered in the shepherds. The first leaders of Israel,

Abraham, Isaac and Jacob, were all shepherds, as was Moses, and not least King David. Even God was regarded as being the 'Shepherd of Israel' (Psalms 23:1). So there is a royal significance in the announcement of the birth of Jesus to shepherds.
- The message of the angel contains three important titles given to Jesus (see chapter 8).
  (a) Deliverer (that is, Saviour). This is a title used only by Luke. Salvation is one of the main themes of his Gospel.
  (b) Christ. Jesus is the Christ, the anointed one of God. He is the one who fulfils all Jewish hope. He will establish the reign of God on earth.
  (c) Lord. This is the title that means that Jesus is king over all creation. The title was used of Jesus after the resurrection.
- Some scholars see, in the reference to the 'heavenly host', the Old Testament idea of the angelic attendants of God: 'Where were you when I laid the earth's foundations? . . . when all the stars of the morning were singing with joy and the sons of God in chorus were chanting praise?' (Job 38:4, 7).
  This singing with joy gives 'Glory to God' and gives 'peace for men who enjoy God's favour'. The whole account shows wonder at the birth of the child in Bethlehem.

The Circumcision and Presentation of Jesus (Luke 2:21–40)

There were three ceremonies required by the Jewish law after the birth of a child.

Circumcision

The story of Jesus' circumcision is very brief. The only significance is that the child is given the name Jesus, which means 'God is salvation'.

Presentation

Mary and Joseph take Jesus to the Temple to present him to God as required by Jewish law (Exodus 13:1–16). The law said that every first-born male should be consecrated to God. In this act, Luke is saying that God, who sent Jesus to do his work on earth, now consecrated him for that work.

Purification

The mother had to be purified because she was considered to be unclean. The ceremonial of the law required it. She had to make a sacrifice. Luke says that, in her case, the offering was laid down for the poor:

> a pair of turtle doves or two young pigeons (*Luke 2:24*).

This once again associates Jesus with the poor.

While Mary and Joseph are in the Temple, a holy man called Simeon takes Jesus in his arms to bless him. Simeon longed for the coming of the Christ and believed he would not die until he had seen him. His view of the Christ is summed up in the divine song called the 'Nunc Dimittis' (Luke 2:29–32). Luke draws once again from the Old Testament, summarising the thoughts of Isaiah (Isaiah 46:13; 49:6; 52:10).

THE MESSAGE OF THE 'NUNC DIMITTIS'

- Simeon has seen the Christ with his own eyes.
- The Christ will offer salvation to all nations.
- This offer will be to the Gentiles as well as the Jews.

This is called *universalism*. It is a favourite theme of Luke's Gospel.

After blessing Joseph and Mary, Simeon made a strange prophecy:

> This child is destined to be a sign which men reject; and you too shall be pierced to the heart. Many in Israel will fall and rise again because of him, and thus the secret thoughts of many will be laid bare (*Luke 2:35*).

These are difficult words to understand. In them Luke attempts to summarise the whole life and work of Jesus.

(a) His life will force all people to decide where they stand regarding himself.

(b) Each person will have to face the fact of their own sinfulness and this will reveal one's secret thoughts.

(c) Those who recognise their need of God will be brought to new life.

(d) The word used for 'rise' is the one Luke uses only for resurrection. It is Luke's intention to show that the rising of a person to new life in Christ will be completed in the resurrection of the Lord after his life has been 'a sign which men reject'.

The story of Jesus' birth comes to an end with Anna, a prophetess who, like Simeon, looked forward to the liberation of Jerusalem and the coming of the Messiah.

The family finally returns home to Nazareth where Jesus grows strong in wisdom and

>   God's favour was upon him (*Luke 2:40*).

The Boy Jesus in the Temple (Luke 2:41–52)

The first twelve years of Jesus' life are passed over in silence. Luke then records a story about Jesus visiting the capital city for the feast of Passover at the age of twelve.

The Jewish law required all faithful Jews to make the pilgrimage to Jerusalem three times a year for three different feasts:

1. The feast of the Passover which called to mind the Exodus, the greatest event in Jewish history when Moses led the children of Israel out of Egypt.
2. The feast of Pentecost which remembered the agreement God made with his people during the wanderings in the desert of Sinai, after their escape from Egypt.
3. The feast of Tabernacles which reminded the children of Israel how they had wandered in the desert and lived in tents (tabernacles), protected and guided by God.

By the time of Jesus, those Jews who lived a good distance from Jerusalem were required only to make the pilgrimage at Passover.

On this occasion Mary and Joseph are on their way home before they realise that Jesus is missing. They return to Jerusalem to search for him.

Luke shows how the close relationship between God and Jesus was already forming in the twelve-year-old. When at last his parents find him sitting among the teachers in the Temple, they ask him what he is doing. Jesus replies:

>   Did you not know that I was bound to be in my Father's house? (*Luke 2:49*).

The story ends with a further comment on the growth of Jesus. In all respects, he continued to grow in wisdom, being prepared for the work that lay ahead of him.

The importance of the birth of Jesus for Christians today

The importance of the birth of Jesus for Christians cannot be overestimated. They believe that in and through Jesus, God became man. He was born like us. This is what the word 'incarnation' means. This is a mystery which some people, in every age, have found difficult to accept.

The best way of saying what Christianity believes about the incarnation is to look at three views which the Church has always refused to accept since the earliest times.

1   Jesus was not God

Some people claim that Jesus was not God. There is only one true God. Jesus, while he was a great and good man, could not possibly be God. This view was first suggested by a priest called Arius, early in the fourth century. It has been suggested many times since.

The Christian Church has always refused to accept this idea. To Christians, Jesus is 'God from God, light from light . . . one in substance with the Father' (Nicene Creed). In other words, in Jesus, God really appeared on earth as a person.

2   Jesus the man and Jesus the Son of God are two different people

The second view unacceptable to Christians is that the Jesus who lived and walked on earth 2000 years ago is not the same person who is called 'Son of God', and who is with God the Father. This view, named Nestorianism after Bishop Nestorius who lived in the fifth century, is still hinted at today. A lot of people seem to refer to Jesus as a good man who lived a long time ago; a man who taught about God and who became 'Son of God' by his resurrection.

The Christian Church rejects this idea. To Christians, Jesus the Christ was and is, always, only one person. God is in the man Jesus at all times.

3   Jesus was God pretending to be a man

The third idea unacceptable to Christians is that Jesus was not really a man at all but God play-acting at being a man. Jesus therefore only acted as if he was a man. God lived on earth only in the outward appearance of a man.

The Christian Church has always rejected this idea. Christians believe that Jesus had not only a human body but also a human mind and spirit. He was fully human as well as fully divine. The real God appeared in a real man.

Saviour, Christ and Lord

Christians believe that God entered the world in Jesus at Bethlehem. He was born to Mary in the outhouse of the inn. All Christians would accept the claims of Matthew and Luke.

- *Jesus is the one who saves people from their sins* – Saviour.
- *Jesus is the Anointed One, the Messiah, the long-awaited representative of God who has and will establish the kingdom of God on earth. He is the new Moses who leads his people from slavery to sin to the freedom of lives lived with God* – Christ.
- *Jesus is king of all people and all creation* – Lord.

Study Skills

Knowledge

1. Who was the Roman Emperor at the time of Jesus' birth?
2. What was the message of the angle to Joseph about the birth of Jesus?
3. What does the word 'Immanuel' mean?
4. What words of greeting did the angel give to Mary when he visited her in Nazareth?
5. What was the message of the angel to Mary?
6. Why did Mary and Joseph have to travel from Nazareth to Bethlehem?
7. What message did the angel give the shepherds the night Jesus was born?
8. What gifts did the wise men present to the baby Jesus?
9. According to Matthew, why did Herod intend to kill all the children of two years old or less?
10. To where did Joseph, Mary and Jesus escape from Herod?
11. Who succeeded Herod the Great as ruler of Judaea?
12. What had Simeon been promised he would see before he died?
13. Which Jewish feast did Jesus celebrate with his parents in Jerusalem when he was twelve years old?
14. Name three canticles or sacred songs in the birth stories of Luke's Gospel.
15. What was Jesus doing when his parents found him in the Temple at the end of their search for him?

Understanding

16. What do you understand to be the meaning of Luke's story of the announcement of the conception of Jesus to Mary; and of Matthew's story of the announcement of the conception of Jesus to Joseph?
17. 'Today in the city of David, a *deliverer* has been born to you – the *Messiah*, the *Lord*'. What is the meaning of this message? Comment especially on the three words in italic.
18. 'In Matthew's birth stories, Jesus shared similar experiences with Moses.' What do you understand these words to mean?

Evaluation

19. How important is the birth of Jesus to an understanding of Christianity today?

20 'Today many people have taken the Christ out of Christmas.' Do you agree with this statement? Give reasons for your answer.

Practical Work

- Write a short nativity play for radio, based on either Matthew's or Luke's Gospel.
- Design two posters/pictures/charts showing the similarities and differences in both the announcement of the birth and the birth of Jesus itself in Matthew's and Luke's Gospels.

CHAPTER

3 The Parables and their Meaning for Today

The parables found in the Synoptic Gospels come from four sources:
  (a) Markan parables: all but one of these are used by both Matthew and Luke.
  (b) 'Q' parables: these are found in both Matthew and Luke but not in Mark.
  (c) 'M' parables: these are found only in Matthew.
  (d) 'L' parables: these are found only in Luke.
The purpose of this chapter is to look at some of the parables found in these four sources. The following topics will be examined:

– What is a parable?
– What is an allegory?
– Why did Jesus use parables?

– Some Lukan parables and their meaning for today
  1 The Parable of the Good Samaritan (Luke 10:25–37)
  2 The Parable of the Rich Man with the Barns (Luke 12:13–21)
  3 The Parable of the Lost Sheep, the Lost Coin and the Lost Son (Luke 15:1–32)
  4 The Parable of the Pharisee and the Tax-collector (Luke 18:9–14)

– The kingdom of Heaven

– Some parables of the kingdom of Heaven
  1 The Parable of the Sower (Matt. 13:4–9, 18–23)
  2 The Parable of the Darnel (Matt. 13:24–30, 36–43) and the Parable of the Dragnet (Matt. 13:47–50)
  3 The Parable of the Mustard Seed (Matt. 13:31–32) and the Parable of the Yeast (Matt. 13:33)
  4 The Parables of the Treasure and of the Pearl (Matt. 13:44–46)
  5 The Parable of the Ten Bridesmaids (Matt. 25:1–13)
  6 The Parable of the Bags of Gold (the Talents) (Matt. 25:14–30)

What is a Parable

A parable is a simple story with a single, simple meaning. It has one central point of teaching and the details of the story make that point both clear and vivid. The meaning is not explained but is left for the listeners to work out for themselves. True parable relates to real life. They have a Palestinian background. The events and characters are drawn from everyday life. Parables are one of the methods of teaching Jesus used.

What is an Allegory?

In contrast, an allegory is a story where the message is hidden in a type of code; where the characters and/or events really represent other characters and events; a story where every detail has a meaning. An allegory may depart from everyday life into a make-believe world. The story has to be decoded in order to understand its meaning.

Some scholars believe that the allegories or allegorical interpretation of the parables were the creation either of the early Christians, or of the Evangelists themselves, reflecting the belief of the churches for whom they were writing.

Why did Jesus use Parables?

1 Parables are simple stories, easy both to listen to and understand.
2 The Jews were used to listening to parables as this method of teaching was well established in their culture.
3 At a time when most learning was by word of mouth, the short story was easily remembered.
4 The hearers have to interpret the parables for themselves. This gave them a deeper meaning and importance. The interpretation became part of a person's experience.

The Evangelists' Answer to why Jesus used Parables

There is, however, an answer given by all three Evangelists to the question, why did Jesus teach using parables? The answer is a very hard one to understand.

They claim that the reason Jesus taught in parables was to confuse people:

> It has been granted to you to know the secrets of the kingdom of Heaven; but to those others it has not been granted . . . That is why I speak to them in parables; for they look without seeing, and listen without hearing or understanding. There is a prophecy of Isaiah which is being fulfilled for them: 'You may

hear and hear, but you will never understand; you may look and look, but you will never see. For this people's mind has become gross; their ears are dulled, and their eyes closed. Otherwise, their eyes might see, their ears hear, and their mind understand, and then they might turn again, and I would heal them (*Matt. 13:10–15*).

This is a problem. The verses seem to be saying that the disciples understand because they have been given the secrets of the mystery of the kingdom but everybody else is taught in parables so that it will confuse them and prevent them coming into the kingdom.

The reason Jesus used parables cannot be to hide the truth from people because this is not the intention of teaching and it seems out of character with what we learn about Jesus elsewhere in the Gospel. There must be another answer to this problem. Various suggestions have been made.

1. The verses are meant to explain the fact that the disciples responded to Jesus, but there were many who refused to repent and stand outside because they did not recognise who Jesus was.
2. The early Christians believed that it was God's plan for the Jews to reject Jesus so that his death and resurrection could unite all people with God.
3. The verses were added to explain why the early Church's teaching was rejected by the Jews.

It would seem that the most likely explanation is that the Evangelists believed the purpose of the parables was to hide the truth from those whose hearts were already set against Christianity. In so doing, they have given a false picture of Jesus' own intention in the use of parables.

Some Lukan Parables and their Meaning for Today

The Parable of the Good Samaritan (Luke 10:25–37)

This parable arises from a question asked of Jesus by a lawyer who was trying to test him. The original question the lawyer asked was

Master, what must I do to inherit eternal life? (*Luke 10:25*).

Jesus answered by asking a question in return. He asked the lawyer to tell him what the Law said. The lawyer made a good reply. To win

eternal life one must love God and love one's neighbour. He was congratulated on his answer by Jesus.

The lawyer, however, still wished to win his argument and asked a second question,

> Who is my neighbour (*Luke 10:29*).

Jesus replied with the Parable of the Good Samaritan.

A man on his way to Jericho was attacked, robbed and left for dead. Both the Priest and the Levite went by without helping him. It was not that they were insensitive or evil men. The Law prevented them from helping. To touch a dead man or to come into contact with the blood of an injured person would make them unclean and mean that they could not carry out their duties. They put the claims of the Law first. The Samaritan stopped, helped and rescued the unfortunate traveller.

The parable concludes with Jesus making the lawyer admit that the Samaritan had been a good neighbour.

Meaning

The answer of the lawyer to Jesus' question about what the Law said deserved the congratulations of Jesus. The two great principles of the kingdom of God are to love God and to love one's neighbour. The parable itself has a clear single meaning. If obedience to the Law takes precedence over human need then there is something wrong with the Law. The true definition of neighbour is anyone in need, irrespective of religious, racial, social or any other division.

The meaning of the parable for today

Christians see, in this parable, the command to treat every individual human being as a neighbour. There can be no room for prejudice in dealing with people. It is true that history records frequent occasions when this has been forgotten and prejudice has shown itself in religious, racial and class distinctions. Christians would claim this is totally foreign to true Christianity. The claims of the kingdom of God dictate that all people must be treated the same and be held in the same esteem.

The Parable of the Rich Man with the Barns (Luke 12:13–21)

On one occasion Jesus is surrounded by a large crowd. A man asks Jesus to tell his brother to divide the property between them. It was quite common in Judaism for an appeal to be made to a religious leader in matters of legal inheritance. Jesus refused the role of

arbitrator. Instead he gave two warnings:
To the poor he said:

> Be on your guard against greed of every kind . . . (*Luke* 12:15)

To the rich he said:

> . . . wealth does not give life (*Luke 12:15*).

Then Jesus went on to tell the Parable of the Rich Man who hoarded his possessions to make sure his future was secure. He retired to enjoy his life. He told himself he could take life easy:

> eat, drink, and enjoy youself (*Luke 12:19*).

That night he died and was parted from his wealth.

Meaning

There are two basic meanings to be found in this parable.

1. There is a warning against greed. Wealth does not restore a person to God.
2. Originally the parable was a story which warned against the coming catastrophe of the end, when a person may be faced with either personal death or the end of the world. The early Church saw, in the parable, a warning to be faithful in the interim period prior to the Second Coming. They thought the day of God's judgment was near when an account would be required of their discipleship.

The meaning of the parable for today

Both these meanings are seen as important to Christians today. Many would claim that the teaching of Jesus is still relevant and that it is virtually impossible to be totally committed to amassing wealth and to serve God at the same time. Many Christians also see life as an important preparation for death. They see eternity in terms of the response made to God while on earth. In addition to this, no one can forecast the moment of death. It can come at the least expected time as, indeed, can the end of the world and the Second Coming of Jesus.

The Parables of the Lost Sheep, the Lost Coin and the Lost Son (Luke 15:1–32)

Jesus told these three parables because, once again, he had been criticised by the Pharisees and Doctors of the Law for mixing with sinners.

The doublet of the Lost Sheep and the Lost Coin are simple in form. Both rely on something lost being found, a sheep in the first parable and a silver coin in the second.

The Parable of the Lost Son is much more involved but still follows the same principle that the son who was lost is found again. Unlike the lost sheep and the lost coin, the son is lost through his own deliberate choice. The parable has certainly allegorical elements about it:

The lost son = the sinner
The father = God
The elder son = the Scribes and Pharisees

The lost son

(a) He squandered his money on the indulgence of all his desires. He became a sinner.

(b) When he had spent all his money he found himself alone and destitute. He sold himself to a local pig farmer. Pigs are 'unclean' to the Jew. This detail in the story shows that the son was driven to the depths of despair. He sat amongst the pigs, so hungry that he was tempted to eat the pigs' swill. He experienced what sin does to a person. He felt completely separated from life.

 Then he came to his senses . . . (*Luke 15:17*).

(c) The young man had reached the lowest point of despair. He knew he was a sinner. He knew he deserved nothing and so he decided to go home and throw himself on his father's mercy.

(d) He returned home rehearsing what he would say to his father.

Meaning

This is a wonderful illustration of how a person strays from God and from his fellow human beings. His actions result in him being utterly and completely lost. This is what sin does to a person.

The father

(a) On his way home the son did not believe that there was any possibility of his father forgiving him. He was relying on the hope that he might, at least, become a servant back in his father's house. He did not expect forgiveness.

But while he was still a long way off . . . (*Luke 15:20*).

(b) The father had never stopped loving his son. Anxiously, he spent the days watching and waiting, constantly looking down the road, longing for his return. At last he saw him and ran to meet him and joyfully welcomed him. The son did not even get chance to finish his prepared speech. The father cut him off in mid-sentence in his eagerness to forgive:

> Quick! fetch a robe, my best one, and put it on him; put a ring on his finger and shoes on his feet (*Luke 15:22*).

The symbols of sonship were restored without reservation.

> For this son of mine was dead and has come back to life; he was lost and is found (*Luke 15:24*).

Meaning

Most people see in the actions of the father a picture of God's forgiveness. Jesus is saying that God forgives the sinner absolutely. There are no conditions attached. God longs for all people to come to him like the son returned to the father in the parable.

The elder son

(a) The elder son was working for the father as usual. When he heard that his brother had returned and had been welcomed back he was angry. After all, his brother had wasted all his money 'with his women'. He deserved nothing.

(b) The father pleaded with the elder brother and tried to point out to him that it was only right to celebrate for it was as if the younger son had come back to life from the dead.

Meaning

Some people feel a certain sympathy with the elder son. He had slaved away. He had been obedient and had never received the fuss that was being made over the return of his brother. He shows the typical standard of human forgiveness and in so doing mirrors exactly the attitude of the Pharisees and Scribes to the poor and outcast of Jesus' day. The forgiveness they offered fell far short of what God required.

These three parables are about the kingdom of God. The kingdom is one in which a forgiving father offers people a chance to return to him. The Judaism of the Pharisees and Scribes did not care for the lost.

The meaning of the parables for today

Christians see, in the three parables of the lost, a picture of God's forgiveness. He does not hold sin against people.

They also claim that forgiveness produces reconciliation only when it is preceded by repentance. God forgives without conditions, but forgiveness is only effective when, like the younger son, a person realises the need to be forgiven.

The Parable of the Pharisee and the Tax-collector (Luke 18:9–14)

The understanding of this parable hinges on the extreme contrast made between the two characters, the Pharisee and the tax-collector.

THE PHARISEE	THE TAX-COLLECTOR
Made people aware of his presence by standing up in full view of everybody in the Temple.	Stood at the back of the Temple, his eyes downcast.
Boasted to God about his goodness in fasting and giving of tithes.	Confessed his failings to God and acknowledged the fact that he was a sinner.
Belittled, sarcastically, all who were not like him, especially the tax-collector.	Refrained from any criticism of others.

The Pharisee's words are not even a prayer. They are merely arrogant words in praise of himself. In contrast the tax-collector shows true humility as he comes to God in prayer. He is the one who is reconciled to God.

Meaning

The parable is teaching that prayer must be offered with the right spirit. This spirit must be one of humility that recognises dependence on God. In this way reconciliation to God can take place.

The meaning of the parable for today

Christians would claim that this parable is at the very heart of the meaning of prayer. There is no place for boastfulness before God. Prayer must be approached in the right spirit of humility.

Study Skills

Knowledge

1   What is a parable?

2 What is an allegory?
3 Give two reasons why Jesus might have used parables.
4 Which parable did Jesus tell in answer to the question, 'Master, what must I do to inherit eternal life?'
5 Who were the two characters who 'went by on the other side' in the Parable of the Good Samaritan?
6 What did God say to the man in the Parable of the Rich Man with the Barns?
7 Name two parables Jesus told in answer to the criticism that he welcomed sinners and ate with them.
8 In the Parable of the Lost Son, how did the younger son squander his money?
9 When did he come to his senses?
10 In the Parable of the Pharisee and the Tax-collector, what was the difference between the two in their attitudes to prayer?

Understanding

11 What do you understand the attitude of Jesus to be towards the outcast and sinner as highlighted in the Lukan parables?
12 Explain the meaning of:

   (a) the Rich Man with the Barns;
   (b) the Lost Coin;
   (c) the Pharisee and the Tax-collector.

Evaluation

13 What do you think is the significance of the three main characters in the Parable of the Lost Son for Christians today?

The Kingdom of Heaven

The theme of many of the parables is the central theme of the Gospel: the meaning of the kingdom of Heaven. ('Kingdom of Heaven' is the term preferred by Matthew. Both Mark and Luke use the term 'kingdom of God'.)

The Jews used the phrase 'kingdom of God' to refer to the power and authority of God. They never used it to mean an earthly kingdom in the sense of an area of land which was ruled by God.

It was more a question of belonging to God's kingdom by responding to him in faith and accepting his 'rule' over one's life.

The Jews looked at the kingdom of Heaven in two different ways:

1 The kingdom of Heaven was *present* in the sense that God guided his people at all times.
2 The kingdom of Heaven will come in the *future* in the sense that God will be accepted by the whole world and his rule will be established on the earth.

The Jews believed that God controlled everything: the forces of nature, Israel as his chosen people and also the destiny of all other nations.

They looked forward to that future time when God's rule would be all over the earth. Some of them believed that it would be brought about by an ideal representative of God, an anointed one, a Messiah (see chapter 8). Jesus says such a moment has arrived.

The first words of Jesus in Luke's Gospel show how Jesus claims to be the anointed one. He quotes the prophet Isaiah:

> The Spirit of the Lord is upon me because he has anointed me (*Luke 4:18*).

The anointed one was to bring

> ... good news to the poor,
> to proclaim release to captives and sight for the blind; ...
> to proclaim the year of the Lord's favour ... (*Luke 4:17–19*).

which is another way of saying, 'proclaim the kingdom of Heaven'. Jesus went on to say that what Isaiah had prophesied has come true. It had come true in Jesus himself.

The meaning of the kingdom of God for today

The idea of the kingdom of Heaven is still relevant to Christians even though the term is not widely used today. They still believe that the kingdom of Heaven is something present in the lives of men and women.

Some say that to belong to the kingdom of Heaven is the same as belonging to the Church.

Others claim that to belong to the kingdom of Heaven is not exactly the same as being a member of the Church. Being a member of the kingdom goes beyond simply belonging to any individual Church. They believe the kingdom of Heaven is to do with the whole person. It is the dedication of the whole of life to God.

The parables of the kingdom, therefore, are still seen as relevant today by all Christians. They may be set in the everyday life of 2000 years ago and, therefore, seem somewhat remote from modern times but the meaning of them is still true.

Some Parables of the Kingdom of Heaven and their Meanings for Today

The Parable of the Sower (Matt. 13:4–9, 18–23)

The Parable of the Sower is one of the most well known of all the parables. The seed falls on four different types of soil: the footpath, rocky ground, among thistles and on good soil. At first sight this may be seen as careless farming with so much seed being wasted.

The parable, however, only makes sense when seen against the method of farming followed in Palestine at that time. Certainly some seed was wasted but this is exactly what used to happen. The sowing was done before the ploughing.

Meaning

A few verses later, after the account of the parable, Matthew gives an allegorical meaning (Matt. 13:18–23). But what would the interpretation be if that allegorical answer were not printed for all to see? There would be a simple parable which shows, on the one hand, the frustrations of the sower's labouring, with its weeds, greedy birds and rocky ground, and on the other hand, in contrast to this, a picture of a rich harvest.

The meaning of this simple story is that the kingdom of God will be successful in spite of all frustrations and difficulties.

The allegorical interpretation of the parable is given in the Gospel. There are four such different kinds of soil representing four types of hearer of the message of Jesus.

1. *The unresponsive hearer*
   Satan carries off the word giving the person no chance to respond.
2. *The shallow hearer*
   The person who has no roots, lacking depth and persistence.
3. *The worldly hearer*
   The person who is seduced by the pleasures of the world.
4. *The responsive hearer*
   The person who, living a life of faith, obtains depth, according to his or her faith.

There is something very unsatisfying about this explanation of the parable. Many scholars believe that this interpretation is not original and was not given by Jesus. They believe that the interpretation is from a later period of the Church and that it arises from using the parable for teaching purposes.

Under self-examination, a person is required to ask, 'What kind of soil am I?' Such an interpretation misses the original and simple truth of the parable.

The meaning of the parable for today

- *The Parable of the Sower is still relevant today. There have been many times in history when Christianity has faced extreme difficulty.*

> Sometimes it has been persecution or suppression. At other times it has been treated with apathy. Throughout, the kingdom of God has not only survived but flourished. Christians of all nations and of every colour and race have found faith in Christ to be the centre of their lives.
- *The allegorical interpretation of the parable also continues to have meaning. The comparison of people with different types of soil may seem strange today but the idea of examining one's own faith is a good one. Christians need to reflect from time to time on their faith, knowing that it is easy to be distracted from their calling to be disciples.*

The Parable of the Darnel (Matt. 13:24–30, 36–43) and the Parable of the Dragnet (Matt. 13:47–50)

The Parable of the Darnel is quite straightforward. A farmer sowed good seed in his field but, while he was asleep, an enemy sowed darnel amongst the wheat. Darnel is a weed, sometimes referred to as 'tares', and has a resemblance to wheat. The farmer's servants were all for pulling out the weeds but the farmer pointed out that this would mean that some of the good wheat would also be lost. He said that both good and bad alike should remain until the harvest.

The Parable of the Dragnet is intended to complement the Parable of the Darnel. This time the illustration is taken not from farming, but from another common industry: fishing. The method of fishing employed was to secure one end of the dragnet on the shore and the other on the boat. The boat would then sail in a circle, dragging the net, until it returned to the point of departure. Then the nets would be hauled in. This method of catching fish was an early form of modern-day trawling.

Meaning

The meaning of the parable itself seems to be that there is a need for patience in the kingdom of Heaven. If the kingdom of Heaven is interpreted as the Christian community in Matthew's Gospel, then the plea for patience applies to the community itself. It would spell disaster in the Christian community to attempt to achieve a pure society in which there were no sinners. Judgment of good and bad is the responsibility of God.

So the parable envisages a situation that could arise in the early Church and advises that human judgment makes mistakes.

As with the Parable of the Sower, Matthew includes an allegorical interpretation of the parable. The explanation of the allegory is:

> the sower ...... = the Son of Man (Jesus)
> the field .... = the world

> the good seed....... = the children of the kingdom
> the darnel .... = the children of the evil one
> the enemy............ = the Devil
> the harvest........... = the end of time
> the reapers........... = the angels

The allegory extends the idea of the parable. With its doublet parable of the dragnet, it tells of the time of final judgment when, at the end of time, the

> Son of Man will send out his angels, who will gather out of his kingdom everything that causes offence (*Matt. 13:41*).

Once again, many scholars believe that this allegorical interpretation is not original and was not given by Jesus. Certainly it misses the simple truth of patience. They believe the interpretation is from the period of the early Church and looked forward to the end of the world.

The meaning of the parables for today

- *These two parables are still relevant today. There have been times when the Church has persecuted even its own people who have held differing views. Certain Christians have also given the impression that they sit in judgment over others. Both such actions have no place in Christianity. Patience, which is born out of tolerance and mutual respect, while still remaining firm in belief, is still the calling of the Christian.*
- *The allegorical interpretations are concerned with the end of the world when Jesus will come again. Many Christians believe that there will be a time in the future when Jesus, as Son of Man, will return. At that time he will establish God's kingdom for all to see. It will be undeniable and unmistakable. Such an event will involve judgment.*

The Parable of the Mustard Seed (Matt. 13:31–32) and the Parable of the Yeast (Matt. 13:33)

These two parables are, in many ways, the simplest of all the parables. The mustard seed is the smallest seed of all, but when it is planted it grows into a tree. The mustard seed produces a shrub about eight to ten feet tall, with branches strong enough to support birds and give them shelter.

The example of the yeast follows the same pattern. Matthew says that a small amount of yeast added to 'half a hundredweight of flour' produces a dough that will rise well beyond its former size. Even though Matthew seems to exaggerate in talking of half a hundredweight of flour, the principle of yeast increasing the size of dough still stands.

Meaning

It is exactly the same with the kingdom of Heaven. From small beginnings it will grow into a vast kingdom of God.

These were common metaphors for a great kingdom to be established by the Messiah. Jesus gathered a small band of followers and, through God's power, they were to become the people of God in the kingdom of God.

The meaning of the parables for today

The Parables of the Mustard Seed and the Yeast can be seen as being in the process of fulfilment. From the beginnings of Christianity in the first century, the movement has continued to spread until it now embraces every continent on earth. From these small beginnings it has grown into something large. Christians believe the growth will continue until the daily prayer which Jesus taught his disciples becomes a reality: 'Your kingdom come! Your will be done on earth as it is in heaven.'

The Parables of the Treasure and of the Pearl (Matt. 13:44–46)

These two simple parables follow the same theme. The first tells of a man who found some buried treasure in a field. He buried it again and then went away and realised enough capital to buy the field so that he could claim the treasure.

The second tells of a pearl merchant who discovered a pearl of rare beauty and again realised his capital to buy it.

Meaning

First of all, it must be noted that these parables are not commending the dishonesty of the man who concealed the true value of the field, or the greed of either man for material possessions. Neither is the important matter in both parables what the two men give up.

The decisive thing is their motive: the overwhelming nature of their respective discoveries. They had discovered the kingdom of Heaven for that is what is compared to both the treasure and the pearl. This discovery filled their hearts with joy but also promoted the most willing and wholehearted sacrifice.

The meaning of the parables for today

Most Christians, if asked about their faith, would include in their explanation the simple joy and happiness that faith has given to them. To belong to God is a gift to all people. To know that they belong to God is, for many Christians, the crowning joy of their lives.

The Parable of the Ten Bridesmaids (Matt. 25:1–13)

This parable is about a Jewish wedding. The bridegroom goes to fetch his bride from her own house. Together, accompanied by the bridesmaids, they return to the bridegroom's house for the wedding and the celebrations that follow. The parable draws a contrast between the bridesmaids, five of whom were wise – ready for the arrival of the bridegroom even though he was late – and five of whom were foolish – unprepared when he finally arrived.

Meaning

Matthew includes this parable as a warning to the Christian community of his own day. They, as members of the kingdom of Heaven, must be ready for the sudden arrival of Jesus at the parousia.

Originally Jesus probably directed this parable against the Jews who were not prepared for the coming of the Messiah and would not accept him.

The meaning of the parable for today

Most Christians believe that there is a time in the future when Jesus will return. They believe that a Christian should be prepared for that return. This does not mean that they should be frightened of punishment. Rather, like the bridesmaids who were prepared and who went to celebrate with joy, the Christian must be ready for Jesus to return. This is a matter of joy for it will mean the celebration of the kingdom of Heaven on earth.

The Parable of the Bags of Gold (the Talents) (Matt: 25:14–30)

The master who went abroad had three servants, each of whom had a certain amount of ability. He divided his capital between the three. To the first he gave five bags of gold, to the second, two bags, and to the third, one bag of gold. The first two traded successfully and increased their master's wealth 100 per cent. The third servant made no attempt to use the gold but dug a hole and kept it safe for his master's return. He took no risks for he was frightened of his master. The first two were rewarded for their success and the third was punished for failing to exercise his stewardship in a proper manner.

Meaning

The parable has two meanings. Originally, it was most probably directed against the Scribes and Pharisees who, like the third servant, had kept the message of God to themselves with their exclusiveness. Considering themselves to be superior, they cared little for the ordinary person and looked down on the sinners.

By the time Matthew wrote his Gospel, the meaning of the parable had changed. The early Church used it as a call to faithfulness and obedience in the interim before the Second Coming of Jesus and the establishing of the kingdom of Heaven over all the earth. Then, when Jesus returns, each person will be required to give an account of their lives and their stewardship.

The meaning of the parable for today

Many Christians see, in this parable, the command to use the talents and abilities they have been given in the service of God and all people. They must not keep such gifts to themselves.

They would admit that this is a very modern interpretation of the parable and that the original meanings of faithfulness and obedience in the time before the parousia are still fundamental to Christian teaching today.

Study Skills

Knowledge

1. List the four types of ground mentioned in the Parable of the Sower. What happened to the seed in each case?
2. Why did the farmer not let his servants pull out the darnel in the Parable of the Darnel?
3. In the allegorical interpretation of the Parable of the Darnel, what do the following represent:

    (a) the sower;
    (b) the field;
    (c) the good seed;
    (d) the enemy;
    (e) the harvest

4. Which, according to the Gospels, is the smallest seed of all?
5. How did the man who found some buried treasure in a field come to own the treasure himself?

6 In the Parable of the Ten Bridesmaids, why were five of them regarded as being foolish?
7 How many bags of gold did the master give to each of his three servants?

Understanding

8 What do you understand by the phrase 'the kingdom of Heaven'? Explain how the parables show that this kingdom is both present and future.
9 What might Jesus have meant by the Parable of the Sower when he first told it? Explain the allegorical meaning that is given in the Gospels.

Evaluation

10 Do you think it is easier to understand parables or allegories? Illustrate your answer with examples from the Gospels.
11 Write a modern parable showing one aspect of the kingdom of Heaven for today.

Examination Practice

Describe briefly the Parable of the Good Samaritan. (4)
What do you think Jesus is teaching in this parable apart from the truth that all people are neighbours? (6)
Name two parables in Luke which use the image of a seed or seeds. (4)
Some people would claim that the parables are out of date and have little to say to a modern world. What are you views? Give reasons for your answer. (6)

Practical Work

- Design a poster or collage showing the following parables:
    (a) the Parable of the Good Samaritan;
    (b) the Parable of the Lost Sheep;
    (c) the Parable of the Pharisee and the Tax-collector.

CHAPTER

4 The Miracles of Jesus in the Synoptic Gospels

The purpose of this chapter is to examine the miracle stories found in the Synoptic Gospels. It is important first of all, however, to look at some questions regarding the approach to this subject.

- What is a miracle?
- Did Jesus perform miracles?
- Why did Jesus heal people?
- The relationship between faith and miracle
- What is faith?
- Exorcisms
- Healing miracles
- Raising from the dead
- Nature miracles

What is a Miracle?

In the twentieth century a miracle is thought of as something extraordinary. It is seen as a direct intervention by God that breaks all the normal laws of nature. It is something that cannot be explained away. Because of this modern definition of miracles many people seem to think miracles do not happen very often today. They are regarded as belonging to an earlier age of superstition and ignorance.

The real meaning of the miracles will be missed if they are treated simply as 'newspaper reports'. The miracles are something much more important. They express the belief that the early Christians had in and about Jesus.

It must be remembered that the Gospel is an expression of Christian belief. Some Christians would say the Gospel is not the source or proof of what happened. So with regard to the miracles, questions such as 'Could this happen?' or 'What happened?' are not the questions to ask. The questions that must be asked about the miracles are:

- Why did the Gospel writers include these stories?
- What did these stories mean to them?
- Do these stories have any importance for Christians today?

Did Jesus Perform Miracles?

There is little doubt that Jesus performed many miracles during his ministry. He is even accused of casting out devils by the power of Satan (Luke: 11:15). Such an accusation is hardly likely to have been invented by his enemies if he had not performed miracles.

Many scholars, however, would doubt whether the accounts in the Gospels are the reports of actual occurrences. In keeping with all the material of the Gospel, the miracle accounts have gone through two separate periods of development. The first is the period of oral tradition when the stories of Jesus were used and passed on by the Church. The second is the influence of the Gospel writers themselves.

As a result of these developments it is possible to make three claims regarding the miracles in the Synoptic Gospels:

1. It is impossible to discover the actual occurrence that stands behind the individual accounts.
2. The accounts, even if they are based on genuine memory as many undoubtedly are, are more examples of the kind of thing Jesus used to do.
3. All the miracles of healing follow a set pattern:
   (a) *Setting*: description of illness, etc.;
   (b) *Cure*: by command, touch or at a distance;
   (c) *Crowd response*: the reaction of the onlookers.

WHY THE STORY WAS REMEMBERED

- The early Church used the miracles to express the belief that God was working among people through the Messiah.
- In this way the miracles show the developing faith of the early Church.
- This development is the result of using the miracle stories in preaching and teaching.

THE EVANGELISTS' USE OF THE STORY

- The Evangelists are responsible for the order in which the material is presented in the Gospels.
- This order of material shows their own beliefs. They use the miracles to illustrate what they want to say about Jesus.

Why Did Jesus Heal People?

Many people would say that Jesus could not stop himself from healing people because of his overwhelming feeling of compassion and love for them. Certainly Christians believe that compassion and love are qualities that Jesus possessed. It should be noted, however, that there are only two miracles where it states that Jesus healed out of a sense of compassion or pity (Mark 1:41; Luke 7:13).

The answer to the question, 'Why did Jesus heal?' can be found in one of the miracles itself. The woman who had a haemorrhage for twelve years, and probably suffered from haemophilia, touched the cloak of Jesus believing that this was all she had to do to be healed. Jesus said to her,

> My daughter, your faith has cured you. Go in peace . . . (*Mark 5:34*).

The older translations have at this point the words: 'Your faith has made you whole.' Jesus wished people to be 'whole', in body, mind and spirit.

This is the real reason for the miracles of healing: to bring a wholeness of life to those in need.

The Relationship Between Faith and Miracle

It is important, however, to understand exactly what the connection is between faith and miracle. Unfortunately, many people today see the miracles as events that make people believe. It is as if they are saying, 'We believe in Jesus because he proved who he was by working miracles.' The reverse is also true. Some people do not believe in Jesus because they do not believe in the miracles. They misunderstand the purpose of the miracles in thinking they are meant to bring about faith. Such people seem to connect miracle and faith like this:

$$\text{MIRACLE} \rightarrow \text{leading to} \rightarrow \text{FAITH}$$

This idea is not the one found in the Synoptic Gospels. It is also not what most Christians believe. Christians throughout history have generally believed in Jesus because of the resurrection not because he performed miracles.

The connection between miracles and faith is quite simple. It is the opposite of what many people think today. Faith comes *before* the miracle. The connection between faith and miracle is:

$$\text{FAITH} \rightarrow \text{leading to} \rightarrow \text{MIRACLE}$$

What is Faith?

Once again, this needs to be clearly stated. Many people seem to have an understanding of faith which borders on superstition. To them Jesus is someone with special powers, almost like a hypnotist, who could place inside a person the belief that he or she could be healed and therefore show faith.

Such a viewpoint is not found in the miracles of the Gospel. Some of the miracles are, for example, performed 'at a distance' where no such psychological relationship could possibly exist (for example, the centurion's servant (Luke 7:1–10)). In the Gospel, faith is seen as an act of trust by which a person relies not on himself or herself but on Jesus. It is an energetic seeking after the power of God. It is the firm belief that he can do something for them through Jesus.

Faith has two main characteristics:

1. It is an *active faith*: a belief that something needs to be done and can be done by this man Jesus. This belief shows itself in *action*:
   e.g. in the cure of the paralysed man (Mark 2:1–12).
2. It is a *praying faith* in the sense of a plea or request. It is a faith that believes it has only to ask in order to receive:
   e.g. in the cure of the leper (Mark 1:40–5).

Faith is the request and miracle is the answer. It is always in that order.

The Church and healing today

The Christian Church still practises healing. Sometimes it is by praying over the sick person. At other times it may be by anointing the sick person with oil. The Church does this because the will of Jesus is that all people should be whole in body, mind and spirit. A person with faith prays for healing in the belief that healing can take place. Sometimes a sick person's friends show their faith in such action as taking a person to a healing service or to some centre of healing such as Lourdes. Faith coming before and bringing about healing is as real to many Christians today as it was at the time of the Gospel.

The miracle stories in the Synoptic Gospels can be divided into four main sections:

- exorcism
- healing miracles
- raising-from-the-dead miracles
- nature miracles

This chapter will look at the following examples:

Exorcisms
The Capernaum demoniac (Mark 1:21–28)
The Gerasene demoniac (Legion) (Mark 5:1–20)
The Syro-Phoenician woman's daughter (Mark 7:24–30)

Healing miracles
The leper (Mark 1:40–45; Luke 5:12–16) and the ten lepers (Luke 17:11–19)
The centurion's servant (Luke 7:1–10)
The woman with the haemorrhage (Mark 5:25–34)
Blind Bartimaeus (Mark 10:46–52)

Raising from the dead miracles
The widow of Nain's son (Luke 7:11–17)
The raising of Jairus' daughter (Mark 5:21–24, 35–43)

Nature miracles
The calming of the storm (Mark 4:35–41; Matt. 8:23–27; Luke 8:22–25)
The feeding of the 5000 (Mark 6:30–44)
The walking on the water (Mark 6:45–52; Matt. 14:22–33)

Exorcisms and their Message for Today

The Capernaum Demoniac (Mark 1:21–28)

An exorcism is the casting out of an evil spirit from a person. The first miracle recorded by Mark is such a casting out of an evil spirit by a direct command.

'Be silent', he said, 'and come out of him' (*Mark 1:25*).

The Jews of Jesus' day believed there were millions of demons about who could possess people, causing illnesses of mind and body and tempting them to sin. Jesus faces such evil and, by the authority he has, commands the evil spirits to go, and they flee.

Why the Story was Remembered

This miracle is remembered by the early Church because it contains the title 'Holy One of God'. The evil spirits recognised Jesus. That is why they called out

What do you want with us . . . have you come to destroy us? (*Mark 1:24*).

The title 'Holy One of God' is found only in this passage in the Gospel of Mark. It is a Messianic title. It means that Jesus is seen as belonging to God in a special way. He is the Messiah.

The evil spirit says, 'Have you come to destroy us?' This suggests that there was more than one. Perhaps this one representative speaks for all the evil spirits. They are all faced with the power of God in Jesus who has come to destroy them.

Mark's Use of the Story

Mark claims that all the people were astonished as they witnessed this contest between good and evil. What is surprising is the comment of the crowd:

> What is this? A new kind of teaching! (*Mark 1:27*).

It is obvious, in this first miracle, that Mark makes no distinction between 'teaching' (Mark 1:21, 22, 27), 'healing' (Mark 1:25, 32–34) and 'preaching' (Mark 1:35–39). All three are part of one and the same mission to offer the kingdom of God to all people. Mark claims that all this is possible because of the *authority* of Jesus:

> He speaks with authority. When he gives orders, even the unclean spirits submit (*Mark 1:27*).

This authority comes from God.

As far as the structure of the Gospel is concerned, it would seem that Mark's purpose in the opening chapter is to show that:

1. Jesus is baptised with the Spirit of God (Mark 1:9–11);
2. Jesus wins the battle against temptation (Mark 1:12–13);
3. Jesus wins the first round in the battle against evil (Mark 1:21–28).

The Gerasene Demoniac (Legion) (Mark 5:1–20)

The place where this exorcism took place differs according to the various translations of the Gospel. There are three alternatives: Gerasene, Gergesene or Gadarene. They are all intended to be the same place: in Gentile country across the Sea of Galilee.

The symptoms of being possessed by an evil spirit are described in detail: an interest in death; abnormal physical strength; insensitivity to pain; and the refusal to wear clothes.

Why the Story was Remembered

A poor man believed himself to be possessed by many devils. His name was Legion. A Roman legion consisted of 6000 men. Legion was very strong. As Mark says,

> He could no longer be controlled; even chains were useless, he had often been fettered and chained up, but he had snapped

his chains and broken the fetters. No one was strong enough to master him (*Mark 5:3–4*).

Yet soon afterwards he sat at the feet of Jesus

clothed and in his right mind (*Mark 5:15*).

Once again evil is powerless when faced with God acting through Jesus.

The miracle is remembered by the early Church because it uses another rare Messianic title: 'Son of the Most High God'. Jesus as Messiah is the 'Son of the Most High God' and as such has power over evil.

One strange feature of the account is the conversation between Jesus and Legion. The evil spirits asked permission to go into the pigs that were nearby. They were given permission and were destroyed as the herd of pigs drowned in the lake. What the early Church believed about this is quite clear. Jesus was concerned to free a human life from the power of Satan, whatever the cost. One human life was more important than a whole herd of pigs.

Mark's Use of the Story

This miracle is placed by Mark just after the chapter on parables in which the secrets of the kingdom of God are given to the disciples. That chapter ends with the calming of the storm where the first hint of 'failure' on the part of the disciples is found. It is interesting that the story of Legion ends on a note of discipleship. Legion wished to be a disciple but Jesus told him to remain where he was in his own district and tell all the people what

... the Lord in his mercy has done for you (*Mark 5:19*).

In this sense Legion was the first missionary figure in the Gospel.

A MODERN DIFFICULTY

Some Christians today have a difficulty with this story. Jesus seemed to have no respect for the livelihood of a Gentile pig farmer. He allowed the herds of pigs to be destroyed. There are three ways of explaining the difficulty:

1. To accept it as being a contest between good and evil (see above).
2. To treat the death of the pigs as a coincidence. It has nothing at all to do with the cure of Legion.

> 3 To say that the death of the pigs did not take place on the same occasion at all and has nothing to do with the miracle. It only became connected with the miracle because both events took place in the same village.

The Syro-Phoenician Woman's Daughter (Mark 7:24–30)

Jesus made one long journey into the north, outside Galilee. He went into the territory of Tyre, in the country called Phoenicia, which was in the Roman province of Syria. Even there it would seem that he was known because a woman came to him and asked him to drive out an unclean spirit from her daughter.

Jesus' reply to the request of the woman to cure her daughter seems very harsh and even rude:

> Let the children be satisfied first; it is not fair to take the children's bread and throw it to the dogs (*Mark 7:27*).

The term 'dog' was used by the Jews to describe the Gentiles.

It has been suggested that Jesus did not mean 'dogs' in the sense of an insult but household dogs who are the family friends. This seems, however, to be a rather weak attempt to soften the harshness of the saying. Other scholars have suggested that Jesus did not make the comment about the dogs. They claim it has been put in the story by the early Church, during the period of the oral tradition, to show that Jesus thought his mission was primarily for the Jews and not the Gentiles. Certainly Luke, who is thought to be writing for Gentiles, omits the story, probably out of respect for his Gentile readers.

The reply of the woman,

> Sir, even the dogs under the table eat the children's scraps (*Mark 7:28*),

shows Jesus that she has faith and her request is granted. The girl is cured even though Jesus does not go to see her.

Why the Story was Remembered

The miracle was remembered by the early Church because of the emphasis on faith. The miracle portrays Jesus as being unwilling to help a Gentile but does so because of the great faith shown by the woman. When a person has faith that Jesus can do something for them, then all things are possible.

Mark's Use of the Story

Mark uses the story to introduce the fact that the message of the Gospel is not only for the Jews but is for everyone regardless of race. This idea is called *universalism*. In curing a Gentile, Mark is stressing the fact that Jesus' power over evil is not witnessed by Jews alone, but extends to all people.

The message of the exorcisms for today

Our twentieth-century idea of illness is different from that of New Testament times. Most illness has a physical cause with physical symptoms. At the time of Jesus these symptoms may have been recognised but the cause would have been unknown. Some exorcisms, for example, describe conditions which today would be thought of as mental illness or, in some cases, epilepsy. There is no suggestion that Christians today view mental illness or epilepsy as the result of being possessed by evil.

It would be foolish, however, to dismiss evil altogether. Many Christians believe that it is possible for a person to be possessed by a force contrary to good; a force called evil.

Study Skills

Knowledge

1 What is an exorcism?
2 Give an example of 'active' faith.
3 Give an example of 'praying' faith.
4 What did the man with the unclean spirit in the synagogue at Capernaum cry out?
5 How does Mark describe Legion's appearance and character?
6 What did Jesus tell Legion to do?
7 In which miracle is Jesus called 'Holy One of God'?
8 Give a brief account of the healing of the Syro-Phoenician woman's daughter.

Understanding

9 What do you understand to be the relationship between faith and miracle?
10 How does our understanding of illness today differ from that at the time of Jesus? Describe, briefly, two miracles that illustrate this difference.

Evaluation

11 Why do you think the miracles of exorcism were remembered by the early Church and recorded by Mark?

Healing Miracles and their Message for Today

The Leper (Mark 1:40–45; Luke 5:12–16) and the Ten Lepers (Luke 17:11–19)

Luke includes two miracles concerning lepers. The first is taken from Mark's Gospel and involves the cure of a single leper; the second is from his own source and is a story about ten lepers. Many scholars believe that the story of the ten lepers is a development of the miracle of the one leper. There are similarities although the emphasis of the second miracle is different.

The details of both healings are scanty. We are not told why the lepers were wandering around when it was normal, at that time, for lepers to be separated from the rest of society. All that is recorded is the two chance meetings between Jesus and lepers. It must be noted that leprosy was not just the twentieth-century disease known by that name but covered many other skin complaints (see Leviticus 13). The Jewish law of separating all those suffering from leprosy from the rest of society was an attempt to stop the spread of contagious disease.

Why the Stories were Remembered

In the first story, Jesus broke the rules and touched the leper. In a moving sentence the account says,

> ... Jesus stretched out his hand, touched him, and said, '... be clean again' (Mark 1:41).

The leper had a 'praying faith' which expressed itself in a plea or request:

> If only you will you can cleanse me (Mark 1:40).

Jesus told the leper to go and show himself to the priest and make an offering for his healing. This was the law. The priest was the only one who could declare a person to be healed from their leprosy.

In the second account, Jesus told them to go and show themselves to the priests, and while they were on their way they discovered they were cured.

In both cases their faith in Jesus had produced healing.

Mark's and Luke's Use of the Stories

The miracle of the single leper is used in two ways:

1. Jesus is seen as fulfilling the Old Testament in the sense that he is greater than the Jewish Law. Illnesses such as leprosy are against God's will and must be defeated.
2. The account is set in a section of the Gospel that shows Jesus' authority. This authority is God given. Jesus is the representative of God.

The emphasis is changed in the second story. The climax of the account is the fact that one of the ten who was cured returns to Jesus to thank him (Luke 17:15). Luke makes the point that he was a Samaritan. Jesus asks what happened to the other nine.

> Could none be found to come back and give praise to God except this foreigner? (*Luke 17:18*).

The fact that the man was a Samaritan highlights the idea of universalism, a major theme of Luke's Gospel.

The message of the miracle for today

For Christians today, the curing of leprosy is not the most important thing about these miracles. The stories show the deeper truth that Jesus comes to people at the point of deepest need. The miracles express both the belief in a God who reaches out and 'touches' – a God who can heal – and also the fact that not only healing but the whole message of Jesus is for all people.

The Centurion's Servant (Luke 7:1–10)

This miracle is set in the town of Capernaum in Galilee. Living in Capernaum was a Roman centurion, who was obviously sympathetic to the Jews and their religion. It was he who had built the synagogue. At first it may seem surprising to find a Gentile so involved in Jewish affairs but it was not all that unusual. There were some Romans who did not believe in all their own pagan gods but who were inclined towards the idea of one universal God. This man had not become a Jew, probably because of his position within the Roman army.

The centurion is also shown to be a compassionate man, for he cares about the health of one of his servants. He sent Jewish representatives to Jesus to ask him to help.

Why the Story was Remembered

This miracle was remembered for three reasons:

1. The healing of the servant was made possible by the prayerful faith of someone other than the sufferer. It is the centurion who has the faith that Jesus can do something.

2. The miracle was performed at a distance. Jesus does not meet the servant. What is even more amazing is that Jesus does not meet the centurion either. The centurion sent word to Jesus that it was not necessary for him to come in person. Jesus only had to say the word and he knew that the servant would be healed (Luke 7:7).
3. The centurion's faith is that Jesus' authority was from God. He explained that, as an officer in the army, he knew that his own commands would be obeyed without question because of his authority. In the same way, Jesus had authority which came from God (Luke 7:6–8).

Luke's Use of the Story

The centurion received, from Jesus, the highest praise given to anyone in Luke's Gospel. He pronounces:

> I tell you, nowhere, even in Israel, have I found faith like this (*Luke 7:9*).

It should always be remembered that the man was a Gentile. This Gentile had professed a faith that no Jew had, believing that Jesus had the authority and power to help. Luke uses this story as the supreme example of his theme of universalism. The Gospel was to be offered to Jew and Gentile alike.

The message of the miracle for today

Christians believe that the good news of the message of Jesus is for all people. It does not depend on race, colour or class. Everyone is the same in the eyes of God, and his love, mercy and forgiveness are for all. The grace of faith is offered to every individual.

The Woman with the Haemorrhage (Mark 5:25–34)

This miracle comes in the middle of the story of the raising from the dead of Jairus' daughter. The woman, who was probably suffering from haemophilia, felt it was necessary to approach Jesus secretly because her illness made her 'unclean' according to the Law. Jesus was aware of her touch even though the crowd were pressing all around him. The touch was the touch of faith. This is an unusual miracle. It is the only one where someone touched Jesus believing that this was all they had to do to be healed. It is important not to interpret the phrase that Jesus had felt some power go out of him as though he were some sort of 'divine energy source' of healing. The words simply mean that Jesus was conscious that someone was seeking his help.

Why the Story was Remembered
It has already been stated that the miracle is important because it gives the clearest reason why Jesus healed. His wish was for a person to 'be made whole'.

Mark's Use of the Story
The Greek verb used in the phrase which is translated 'your faith has cured you' ... (5:34; 8:47) is the verb 'to save'. This verb is used in the Old Testament when it means the salvation of God for his people. The first readers of this Gospel would see, in the story of the woman with the haemorrhage, an illustration of the fact that the time of salvation has arrived in the person of Jesus. In him the spirit of God is at work.

The message of the miracle for today
The wholeness of life is important to all Christians. They believe this to be God's will and that anything that hinders this is contrary to the will of God. Wholeness of body, mind and soul should be the prior concern of all Christians and they believe that this wholeness can be found through faith.

Blind Bartimaeus (Mark 10:46–52)
This is the last miracle in the Gospel. Jesus was on his way to Jerusalem and had reached Jericho. It is here that Bartimaeus, a blind beggar sitting by the side of the road, cried out to be cured of his blindness.

Why the Story was Remembered
The Church remembered this miracle because of the use of a rare title, 'Son of David'. This is a Messianic title. What the miracle is really saying is that the blind man recognises Jesus as the Messiah.

Faith is shown in this miracle in the sense of a plea or request. The cry of the blind man,

> Son of David, Jesus, have pity on me! (*Mark 10:47*),

shows a faith that persists even when he is told to be quiet by the crowd.

Mark's Use of the Story
There are three important things to note about Mark's use of this miracle:

1   . . . your faith has cured you *(Mark 10:52).*

Once again Mark has used the Greek verb 'to save'. God's salvation is offered through Jesus.

2   . . . he . . . followed him on the road *(Mark 10:52).*

The word 'disciple' in Greek means 'to follow'. Bartimaeus became a disciple. This is the only miracle (with the possible exception of the Gerasene demoniac) where the person is known to have become a disciple.

3   Mark places this miracle at the end of the central section of the Gospel. Part of the teaching of the central section is to show how the disciples misunderstood the reason Jesus had come. So, with Bartimaeus becoming a disciple, Mark is trying to show how, through faith, a person might come to understand and see. If one has faith, then salvation is received and discipleship follows:

– *faith* is the *insight*
– *salvation* is the *result*
– *discipleship* is the *way*

The message of the miracle for today

This is the experience of many Christians today. By faith they grow in understanding and insight. They draw near to God by the gift of his salvation and become disciples in their own lives.

The importance of the healing miracles for Christians today: Summary

The importance of the healing miracles for most Christians today is not simply the fact that Jesus performed them. As was stated at the beginning of the chapter, Christianity does not depend on a belief that Jesus worked miracles. Most Christians would take that for granted. The importance of the miracles is the teaching they give about Jesus to the modern Christian. They say something about the faith necessary for Christian belief in Jesus.

1   *Christians believe that Jesus is concerned about their needs and will reach out to 'touch' them and help them –* the leper *(Mark 1:40–45).*
2   *Christians believe that Jesus forgives their sins and that this is an important part of their relationship with him –* the paralysed man *(Mark 2:1–12). (See chapter 5.)*
3   *Christians believe that God's wish is for all people to be complete in body, mind and spirit. Faith in Jesus can produce wholeness of life –* the woman with the haemorrhage *(Mark 5:25–34).*

4 *Christians believe that faith in Jesus is of paramount importance* – the centurion's servant *(Luke 7:1–10)*. *It can lead to a deeper relationship with him which results in being disciples and following his way of life* – blind Bartimaeus *(Mark 10:46–52)*.

Raising from the Dead Miracles

The Widow of Nain's Son (Luke 7:11–17)

This story has no mention of the requirement of faith. It seems to arise out of overwhelming compassion for the poor widow who was in the process of burying her only son.

> When the Lord saw her his heart went out to her, and he said, 'Weep no more' *(Luke 7:13)*.

Why the Story was Remembered

Some scholars believe that this story is more theological than historical. It has overtones of an Old Testament story in which the prophet Elijah also raised a widow's son from death and 'gave him back to his mother' (Luke 7:15; 1 Kings 17:23). This reference of Elijah would have been fully understood by Jewish readers and would also account for the crowd response at the end of the story:

> A great prophet has arisen among us . . . God has shown his care for his people *(Luke 7:17)*.

Perhaps the story was remembered because:

1 It showed that Jesus has a life-giving power no less powerful than that of Elijah before him.
2 More than this, it also indicated that Jesus was greater than Elijah. He is not just a prophet. In the next story in the Gospel, John the Baptist sent some disciples to Jesus to ask if he was the one who was to come or whether they should begin to look elsewhere. The reply of Jesus states clearly that Jesus was more than a prophet. (Luke 7:22–23). He is the Messiah.

Luke's Use of the Story

There can be no disputing the fact that Luke includes this story for one main reason. Not only can Jesus heal people, but he can also conquer death. Death is the symbol of sin and evil but this is no longer a thing to be dreaded. The story is an expression of belief in the power of Jesus.

The message of the miracle for today

Christians still hold this same belief today. They believe that death has been conquered and that it is not the end of life. Many would also say that real life is only possible when one has accepted the finiteness of life on earth as something that God uses to draw people into a closer union with himself. This union is one in which there is no death, only eternal life.

The Raising of Jairus' Daughter (Mark 5:21–24, 35–43)

Jesus had just returned from the country of the Gerasenes. In the crowd that surrounded him was a man called Jairus, who was the president of one of the local synagogues.

Jairus pleaded with Jesus to cure his twelve-year-old daughter who was at home, dying. On the way Jesus cured the woman with the haemorrhage.

Before they could arrive at Jairus' house, a message was received that the daughter had died. Jesus told Jairus not to worry but to have faith. He took Peter, James and John into the house where the girl was surrounded with people crying and wailing in their distress. When Jesus said the girl was only asleep, they all laughed at him.

Jesus took the little girl by the hand and told her to get up. She got up immediately.

Why the Miracle was Remembered

Once again, faith is the key to this miracle. Jairus showed faith; a praying faith in asking Jesus to help. He believed help was possible from Jesus. When the message arrived that the child was dead, the message of Jesus was clear. This was a message not only to Jairus but to the whole Church:

>   Do not be afraid; only show faith (*Mark 5:36*).

Mark's Use of the Story

The main problem with this miracle is the question of whether or not Mark meant it as a healing or a raising from the dead miracle. Jesus said that the child was only asleep. Some people think that Jesus still meant death in the sense that it might be said today that a person had 'fallen asleep' when they had died. It must be noted, however, that Jesus made a point of saying that

>   The child is not dead . . . (*Mark 5:40*).

The Aramaic words 'Talitha cum', meaning 'Get up, little child', are preserved in this story. It is thought that the Christians of the early Church valued such phrases which had been spoken by Jesus and used them in their original Aramaic form.

Whatever the interpretation, it is plain that both Mark and the early Church saw in this story an illustration of the power of God to raise the dead. The message of the miracle is that of a 'parable'. Death is not the end. Life comes after death.

The message of the miracle for today

As with the widow of Nain, the message of the miracle is that death is not the end. Jesus has power over death and new life comes after death.

Nature Miracles

Nature miracles are, for some people today, the most difficult to accept:

1 They seem to be inconsistent with what is known of the laws of nature.
2 They are also inconsistent with the story of the temptation of Jesus where he refused to use his powers to compel belief by spectacular 'proofs'.

They are, however, the only miracles performed without an audience other than the disciples. (Even the feeding of the 5000 seems to pass unnoticed by the crowds. There is no 'crowd respone' at all.) It would seem, therefore, that the nature miracles come from an early disciple source.

Whatever the original miracles were, there can be little doubt that the accounts, as recorded in the Gospel, have been developed from their first historical setting. They now carry deeper theological meanings, which were probably given to them by the Church in the period of the oral tradition.

The Calming of the Storm (Mark 4:35–41; Matt. 8:23–27; Luke 8:22–25)

Sudden storms are quite common on the Sea of Galilee. They tend to subside as quickly as they arise. Standing behind this account is probably one such incident. It is important to compare the accounts of this incident in the Gospels, especially those of Mark and Matthew. Certain differences occur both in words and in the order of events:

1. The word spoken by the disciples when the storm blows are very different:

   Master we are sinking. Do you not care? (*Mark 4:38*).
   Save us Lord, we are sinking! (*Matt. 8:25*).

2. Mark rebukes the winds whereas Matthew questions the disciples:

   Hush! Be still (*Mark 4:39*).
   Why are you such cowards? How little faith you have! (*Matt. 8:26*).

3. Mark rebukes the disciples whereas Matthew rebukes the winds:

   Why are you such cowards? Have you no faith even now? (*Mark 4:40*).
   Then he stood up and rebuked the wind (*Matt. 8:26*).

Mark's and Luke's Use of the Story

Both Mark and Luke treat the miracle almost like an exorcism. Jesus speaks to the wind and sea with words that are very similar to those used in speaking to evil spirits. In the Old Testament the sea was the symbol of chaos and evil, which could only be overcome by God. The question asked at the end of the miracle,

> Who can this be? He gives his orders to wind and waves, and they obey him (*Mark 4:41; Luke 8:25*),

is left unanswered. The answer is obvious. Jesus, acting as God, is the one whom even wind and sea obey. The story is similar to the ideas found in the Old Testament:

'So they cried to the Lord in their trouble,
and he brought them out of their distress.
The storm sank to a murmur
and the waves of the sea were stilled.
They were glad then that all was calm,
as he guided them to the harbour they desired' (Psalms 107:29–30).

Matthew's Use of the Story

Matthew seems to interpret this miracle as an 'allegory'. In the early days of the Church, Christians suffered persecution and had to have great faith to survive the violent opposition they received. This miracle shows a picture of the Church. The boat is the Church and the storm is the persecution of the Church. Those who lose heart and cry out in despair are reminded that Jesus is in command and that he will steer the little ship of the Church into calmer waters. In the meantime they must keep their faith.

The Feeding of the 5000 (Mark 6:30–44)

Once again, it is believed that the disciples were the source of the miracle of the feeding of the 5000. There is an eyewitness comment about the grass being green. This may seem insignificant as, in Britain, the grass is almost always green. This is not so in Palestine where, in high summer, the grass can be more yellow in colour. It is surprising that no crowd reaction to the miracle is given.

Some people have tried to explain away this miracle and have suggested that the crowd merely shared what food they had with them. This sort of explanation completely misses the meaning of the story.

Why the Story was Remembered

The early Church, noting that this miracle took place in the wilderness, 'a lonely place', would have seen a parallel with the feeding of the children of Israel with manna in the wilderness of the Sinai desert. Just as God fed his children in the desert so now Jesus feeds his people in the 'lonely place'.

Also to early Christians the story may have been seen as an anticipation of the Last Supper. Jesus blessed and broke the bread (Mark 6:41). Certainly this is how St John interpreted the story in his Gospel some forty years later (John 6).

Mark's Use of the Story

Mark saw Jesus as the Messiah. The Jews believed the reign of the Messiah would begin with a banquet. In this miracle there is a picture of the Messiah feeding his people. Such a picture points to the great Messianic feast in the future. The Messiah offers salvation; a way into that Banquet.

The Walking on the Water (Mark 6:45–52; Matt. 14:22–33)

Many scholars believe that this miracle has the same root as the calming of the storm. Certainly there are great similarities. It may well be the same story that has come down in two different strands of tradition.

Why the Story was Remembered

As with the calming of the storm, this miracle is an allegory of the early Church facing the problems of persecution. The Church is rowing hard against the mounting waves and winds of persecution and opposition, but is making little headway. It is at that moment that Jesus comes, not as a ghost but as himself, to save them and take away their fear.

Mark's Use of the Story

As in the calming of the storm, Mark saw the sea as being an evil power over which Jesus had control.

The real key to understanding this miracle, however, is in the use of the phrase.

> It is I *(Mark 6:50)*.

The Greek words are 'ego eimi' which is the Greek phrase for the Hebrew *Yahweh,* the divine name of God. Its meaning is 'I am'. Mark intends us to see Jesus in this divine sense, walking on the water as an example of divine authority. The story tells us who Mark believes Jesus to be. He is God.

Mark ends the story by saying that the disciples had not understood this:

> ... they were completely dumbfounded ... their minds were closed *(Mark 6:51–52).*

Matthew's Use of the Story

Matthew alone includes an episode about Simon Peter:

> Peter called to him: 'Lord if it is you, tell me to come to you over the water.' 'Come,' said Jesus. Peter stepped down from the boat, and walked over the water towards Jesus. But when he saw the strength of the gale he was seized with fear; and beginning to sink, he cried, 'Save me, Lord.' Jesus at once reached out and caught hold of him, and said, 'Why did you hesitate? How little faith you have!' *(Matt. 14:28–31).*

Matthew uses the story to teach about faith. Peter stands for the Church under persecution. Their faith is being tested. At all costs they must keep the faith. Matthew is extending here the theme first highlighted in his account of the calming of the storm. The way in which he ends his account, so different to Mark, supports his theme:

> And the men in the boat fell at his feet, exclaiming, 'Truly you are the Son of God' *(Matt. 14:32–33).*

SUMMARY

- The miracle accounts are not historical reports of what happened. They are 'summaries' of the type of thing Jesus used to do.
- Most of the miracles follow a set literary pattern.
- The miracle accounts have been developed both by the early Church and the Evangelists to say something important about Jesus.
- The early Church used miracles to teach who they believed Jesus was: *the Messiah*.
- The Evangelists use the miracles to say who Jesus is but the way they arrange their accounts shows that they are also interested in the *authority* of Jesus, the *salvation* offered by Jesus and Jesus' conquest of evil.
- Luke especially uses the miracles to forward his view on universalism. The offer of Jesus is made to the sick, the poor and the bereaved of every nation, not just the Jews.

Study Skills

Knowledge

1. What did the leper say to Jesus?
2. In which miracle does Jesus touch the person he heals?
3. In which miracle does Jesus not meet either the person he heals or the person who requests the healing?
4. In which miracle is Jesus called 'son of David'?
5. How did Jesus calm the storm?
6. Where was Jesus when he raised the widow's son from the dead?
7. To whom did Jesus say, 'Your faith has cured you'?
8. Who returned to Jesus to thank him after he had been healed?
9. What is the meaning of the words 'Talitha cum'?
10. When Jesus walked across the water to the disciples what did he say to them when he realised they thought he was a ghost?

Understanding

11. What do you understand to be the importance and place of faith in the healing miracles?
12. Explain why nature miracles are, for some people, more difficult to believe than healing miracles.

Evaluation

13 'The miracles were recorded because they comment on the person and work of Jesus.' Do you think this is true? Give examples in your answer.
14 Do you think that the nature miracles have any value in preaching the Christian message today? Give reasons for your answer.

Examination Practice

Describe what happened when Jesus healed the centurion's servant. (5)
What does this miracle teach about faith? (5)
Name two other occasions when a person wishing to be healed showed faith in Jesus. (3)
What would you say to a person who said that miracles do not happen today? (7)

Practical Work

- Produce a chart of the miracles you have studied in this chapter. Make sure that the chart shows:

    (a) the exorcisms;
    (b) the healing miracles commenting on faith;
    (c) the raising from the dead miracles;
    (d) the nature miracles.

- Record on the chart any 'pronouncements' (see chapter 1) that Jesus makes in the miracles.

5 Responses to Jesus

The purpose of this chapter is to look at the varying responses to Jesus found in the Synoptic Gospels. This can be done by examining:

- The response of discipleship
    1. The call of the first disciples (Mark 1:14–20; 2:13–14)
    2. Caesarea Philippi (Mark 8:27–9:1; Matt. 16:13–28)

- The response of the Jewish leaders: Conflict stories and interpretations for today
    1. The authority to forgive sins (Mark 2:1–12)
    2. Eating with sinners (Mark 2:16–17)
    3. Fasting (Mark 2:18–22)
    4. In the cornfields on the Sabbath (Mark 2:23–28)
    5. Healing on the Sabbath (Mark 3:1–6; Luke 6:6–11; 13:10–17; 14:1–6)

- The response of the sinner
    1. In the house of Simon the Pharisee (Luke 7:36–50)
    2. Zacchaeus (Luke 19:1–10)

The Response of Discipleship

The Call of the First Disciples (Mark 1:14–20; 2:13–14)

In the opening two chapters of Mark's Gospel, Jesus calls five men to be his disciples. The first four are called by the lakeside in Galilee (Mark 1:16–20). They were fishermen. Simon and Andrew, his brother, were fishing while the other brothers, James and John, were mending their nets. Jesus told them to leave everything and follow them. He said to Simon and Andrew that they were to become

fishers of men (*Mark 1:17*).

This phrase comes from the prophet Jeremiah and means that the disciples were to bring people back to God.

The other disciple called by Jesus was Levi, the son of Alphaeus. He was a tax-collector who was at work in the customs house by the lakeside. Again Jesus told him to follow and Levi

> rose and followed him (*Mark 2:13–14*).

The surprising thing about these accounts is the way in which the five men responded immediately to the call of Jesus.

There are two important points that Mark wishes to make:

1. Jesus has the authority to call these men in such a way that they respond immediately;
2. Mark reminds his readers that discipleship makes a total demand. Some are called to leave everything and follow, regardless of cost.

Discipleship today

This calling is still evident today. That is what the word 'vocation' means. People who have a vocation to the priesthood, ordained ministry or religious orders are required to turn their backs on personal wishes and commit themselves to God regardless of cost. For some, as in the Roman Catholic Church, this means taking a vow of celibacy; for some entering religious orders it means taking the vows of celibacy, poverty and obedience.

The question of vocation, however, can be more widely applied to the whole question of being a Christian. The Christian considers discipleship to be a vocation. Vocation, therefore, is expressed through the different aspects of life, for example, through marriage, work and relationships with others.

Caesarea Philippi (Mark 8:27–9:1; Matt. 16:13–28)

This story is of great importance to both Mark and Matthew. It is the turning point of the Gospel. Up to this moment, the Messiahship of Jesus had passed almost unrecognised. Then, in response to the question,

> Who do you say I am?

Peter made his profession of faith:

> You are the Messiah (*Mark 8:29*).

(Matthew adds the words:

> the Son of the living God (*Matt. 16:16*).)

At this point Matthew adds further words which only he records:

> Simon son of Jonah, you are favoured indeed! You did not learn that from mortal man; it was revealed to you by my heavenly Father. And I say this to you: You are Peter the Rock; and on this rock I will build my church, and the powers of death shall never conquer it. I will give you the keys of the

kingdom of Heaven; what you forbid on earth shall be forbidden in heaven, and what you allow on earth shall be allowed in heaven (*Matt 16:17–19*).

Simon was given the nickname 'Peter', which means 'rock'. On him the Church was to be built. He was to be the authority, as head of the Church. Peter was given the authority to declare what was to be allowed and accepted in the Church. In this sense he was given the keys of the kingdom of Heaven. But it was an authority *on earth*, and the idea of Peter as some doorkeeper of heaven should be resisted.

This insight of Peter was to be short lived for Jesus began to teach them that his Messiahship was one of suffering. Peter would not accept this and began to argue, only for Jesus to turn on him:

Away with you Satan . . . you think as men think, not as God thinks (*Mark 8:33*).

Jesus then went on to give a very clear indication of the cost of discipleship:

Anyone who wishes to be a follower of mine must leave self behind; he must take up his cross, and come with me (*Mark 8:34*).

Two thousand years after these words were spoken, there is a tendency to water down their meaning. It is important to understand what these words meant originally.

(a) **To leave self behind**. To leave self behind does not just mean denying oneself. It does not mean going without certain pleasures in life like so many people do, for example, in Lent. To leave self behind means to put oneself last in all things; to have no care about one's life, position or esteem; and to have no desire for rights or privileges except that of belonging to God.

(b) **To take up the cross**. Again many people have watered this saying down. They seem to equate the word 'cross' with a burden or anxiety. 'We all have our cross to bear' has become a modern-day expression. To 'take up the cross' was a frightening expression to the early Christians of the first century and to many since in every age. For many Christians of Mark's day, their fate was to die for Christ. Discipleship means being prepared to follow Jesus even to the point of death.

(c) **To come with me**. This command of Jesus' for all people to come with him only makes sense when put into the context of the teaching that immediately comes before it. Jesus has just stated that he had to go through great suffering; to be rejected by the Jewish leaders; and to be put to death and to rise again. The invitation to go with Jesus is an invitation to travel along the same road. Discipleship can involve suffering, rejection and death.

For those who do respond there will be a reward. Just as Jesus will rise from the dead after the suffering and death, so those who accept his challenge to become disciples will find life:

> Whoever cares for his own safety is lost; but if a man will let himself be lost for my sake and for the Gospel, that man is safe (*Mark 8:35*).

The reverse is also true. Those who refuse the challenge to become disciples will find that Jesus does not recognise them as members of the community (Mark 8:38).

Discipleship today

Many Christians today, especially in the Western world, are not called on to bear suffering, rejection and death in their discipleship. It is important, however, to realise that discipleship still involves this sacrifice for some.

In our own century, thousands of Christians have suffered martyrdom for their faith. Hundreds of clergy and laity, both Roman Catholic and Protestant, lost their lives in the Germany of the Third Reich. Many have been killed in the political struggles of South America and in the missionary work in Africa, and many are still persecuted in many communist countries.

The twentieth century has its own Christian martyrs: St Maximilian Kolbe, who exchanged places with a condemned Jew in the concentration camp and was starved along with his fellow prisoners, before being fatally injected with carbolic acid; Dietrich Bonhoeffer, a minister of the Confessing Church of Germany, who was executed by the Nazis; and Archbishop Romero, gunned down when he was at a prayer meeting. For each martyr well known, there are thousands who are little remembered but who suffered death because they were disciples of Christ.

The Response of the Jewish Leaders: Conflict Stories and Interpretations for Today

The Authority to Forgive Sins (Mark 2:1–12)

Originally this miracle was one of faith. The faith, shown by the friends of the paralysed man who carried the stretcher, is an active faith. The details of how they opened up the roof and lowered the man down through the tiles to the feet of Jesus are so vivid that the account obviously has some true foundation to it. It is probably based on an eyewitness account. There are, however, two difficulties with the miracle:

1. In no other passage in Mark's Gospel does Jesus claim to forgive sins.
2. The claim to forgive sins is supported by the miracle. Elsewhere Jesus avoids such claims, and in the story of the temptation Jesus resisted the idea of using miracles to prove who he was, or what he had come to do.

Many scholars suggest that verses 5b–11a are not part of the original tradition from which this account is taken but are a very

---

2:1 When after some days he returned to Capernaum, the news went round that he was at home; 2. and such a crowd collected that the pace in front of the door was not big enough to hold them. And while he was proclaiming the message to them, 3. a man was brought who was paralysed. Four men were carrying him, 4. but because of the crowd, they could not get him near. So they opened up the roof over the place where Jesus was, and when they had broken through they lowered the stretcher on which the paralysed man was lying. 5. When Jesus saw their faith, he said to the paralysed man . . . 11b. 'I say to you, stand up, take your bed and go home.' 12. And he got up, and at once took his stretcher and went out in full view of them all, so that they were astonished and praised God. 'Never before,' they said, 'have we seen the like.'

5b. 'My son, your sins are forgiven.' 6. Now there were some lawyers sitting there and they thought to themselves, 7. 'Why does the fellow talk like that? This is blasphemy! Who but God alone can forgive sins?' 8. Jesus knew in his own mind that this was what they were thinking, and said to them, 'Why do you harbour thoughts like these? 9. Is it easier to say to this paralysed man, "Your sins are forgiven", or to say "Stand up, take your bed and walk?" 10. But to convince you that the Son of Man has the right on earth to forgive sins.' 11. He turned to the paralysed man . . .

early addition by the Church. Such a suggestion makes sense when a comparison is made between the accounts with and without these verses. The account is complete as a simple miracle of healing. The basic reasons for this suggestion are:

1. The early Church believed Jesus was the 'Son of Man' (see chapter 8).
2. The early Church believed Jesus did forgive sins.
3. The early Church believed miracles were proof of who Jesus was.
4. The early Church had to face the charge of blasphemy. This miracle showed that Jesus' claim to forgive sins was not blasphemous.

Interpretation for today

Christians see, in this miracle, the eternal truth that sins can be forgiven and that this forgiveness comes through Jesus. Christians believe that the quality of forgiveness is most important in order to achieve not only personal closeness to God but reconciliation between people.

They believe that Jesus died so that sins might be forgiven, and therefore that this story is an illustration of this truth. Jesus forgives sins.

Eating with Sinners (Mark 2:16–17)

The Problem

The Pharisees and Scribes would not eat with the ordinary people as they considered them to be irreligious. They would have nothing to do with recognised 'sinners' such as tax-collectors because they considered them to be immoral.

Jesus had called Levi to be a disciple. Levi was a tax-collector who worked for the Romans. This was the main reason the Pharisees hated the tax-collectors: they were in the pay of the Romans. Levi, in gratitude to Jesus, gave a party for him and the other disciples, to which a number of Levi's friends were invited. The Scribes (i.e. the Doctors of the Law) and Pharisees complained that Jesus was wrong to eat in such company. They believed that it was wrong because Jesus was mixing with people who were not tolerated by strict Jews. Furthermore, Jesus was probably touching dishes and using utensils that were considered 'unclean'.

The Reply of Jesus

Jesus' reply condemned the Pharisees and Scribes but also explained the purpose of his mission:

> It is not the healthy that need a doctor, but the sick; I did not come to invite virtuous people, but sinners (*Mark 2:17*).

If the Pharisees and Scribes thought themselves to be so perfect that they were not aware of their own sin then little could be done for them. The Pharisees considered themselves to be self-sufficient. They were not open to God. They were blind. They were outwardly religious but their hearts were far from God. Jesus said he came not for such 'virtuous' people but to give hope to those who were aware of their need of God.

Fasting (Mark 2:18–22)

The Problem

Fasting was required from all Jews on the Day of Atonement (the day on which the Jews asked God, by means of sacrifice, for the forgiveness of sin) and on other special occasions such as severe drought or some national crisis. Apart from this, fasting was a personal and voluntary matter. The practice of fasting had grown up amongst the Pharisees as a sign of their superiority. They looked upon it as a practice pleasing to God. By the time of Jesus, the Pharisees fasted on two days of the week, Monday and Thursday.

Jesus' disciples were criticised for not fasting. The fasting mentioned cannot have been the national fast on the Day of Atonement for all Jews kept this fast. It is most likely that it had to do with the extra fasts practised by the Pharisees and in this case the disciples of John the Baptist, who may have been mourning the death of their leader.

The Reply of Jesus

The reply of Jesus makes it clear that the time for fasting had not yet arrived. He used the illustration of the wedding. Nobody fasts at weddings. Jesus compared himself to the bridegroom. While he was still with them it was a time of celebration and joy. The idea of the wedding was taken up by the early Church as an illustration of the glory of the coming of God's kingdom at the end of time. They also saw the bridegroom as an allegorical symbol for Jesus in relation to the Church as the bride.

Jesus goes on to say that the time will come when the bridegroom will be taken away. This means that there will be time to fast after the death of Jesus in the sense that it will be, for a short while, a time of great sorrow.

In the Cornfields on the Sabbath (Mark 2:23–28)

The Problem

The Sabbath laws of the Jews were based on the story of creation in Genesis. God created the world in six days and rested on the Sabbath. So the idea of keeping the Sabbath day holy was born. By the time of Jesus this commandment had been developed into a list of 513 points of law with detailed conditions of each and every possible situation. The law stated, for example, that no work could be done on the Sabbath. Work was carefully defined under thirty-nine headings. Some of the things under the heading of work which was not allowed on the Sabbath were sowing, reaping, threshing, preparing food, spinning, putting out a fire, lighting a fire, carrying a burden and writing two letters of the alphabet.

Jesus and his disciples were accused by the Pharisees of reaping, threshing and eating food prepared on the Sabbath day. All they had done was to pick ears of corn as they walked along, rub them in their hands and eat the grain.

The Reply of Jesus

Jesus, in reply, used a method of argument well known to the Jews. He referred to an Old Testament story in which King David, regarded by the Jews as their greatest king, had broken the law when it was necessary to feed his retreating and hungry troops. Jesus claimed that

> the Sabbath was made for the sake of man and not man for the Sabbath (*Mark 2:27*).

In other words, human need is more important than Sabbath law. Jesus makes one further claim:

> ... the Son of Man is sovereign even over the Sabbath (*Mark 2:28*).

This saying shows that Jesus, as God's representative, had the authority to break the Sabbath law.

Healing on the Sabbath (Mark 3:1–6; Luke 6:6–11; 13:10–17; 14:1–6)

The Problem

The keeping of the Sabbath was extremely important to the survival of the Jewish religion. The book of Genesis tells how God had created the world in six days and commanded the seventh to be a day of rest. No work could be done on the Sabbath. Any threat to the Sabbath day was seen as a threat to the Jewish faith as a whole. Such a threat was bound to meet with opposition.

The Jewish law stated that no healing could take place on the Sabbath day unless it was a matter of life and death. Any non-emergency must wait until the Sabbath was over.

Mark records the miracle of the healing of the man with the withered hand (Mark 3:1–6), while Luke records this miracle (Luke 6:6–11) and two more miracles in addition: the healing of the enfeebled woman (Luke 13:10–17) and the healing of a man with dropsy (Luke 14:1–6). Some scholars think that all three belong to the same basic source, or at the very least two sources. Certainly they contain similar sayings and illustrations.

	Withered arm Mark 3:1–6; Luke 6:6–11	**Enfeebled woman** Luke 13:10–17	**Dropsical man** Luke 14:1–6
Where?	Synagogue	Synagogue	House of Pharisee
Who was watching?	Lawyers and Pharisees	President of the Synagogue	Lawyers and Pharisees
What did Jesus say to them?	'Is it permitted to do good or to do evil on the Sabbath, to save life or to destroy it?'		'Is it permitted to cure people on the Sabbath or not?'
The Cure	'Stretch out your arm' His arm was restored.	'You are rid of your trouble'	He took the man and cured him.
Observers' reaction	They were angry.	He was indignant.	They said nothing.
What did he/they say/do?	Discussed what to do about Jesus.	There are six working days. Cure then, not on the Sabbath	
What Jesus said		Hypocrites. Each of you takes an ox or donkey for water on the Sabbath. Was it wrong to cure the woman?	If a donkey or ox falls into a well on the Sabbath, do you not rescue it?
Final reaction		Opponents confused. People overjoyed.	They could find no reply.

In these three miracles Jesus claimed the right to do any action on the Sabbath that was for the good of people. To heal on the Sabbath was part of that claim.

There is no mention of faith because faith is not an important truth in this narrative. What is important is that Jesus saw that blind obedience to the letter of the law was stopping a man from being healed.

The Church remembered these miracles for two reasons:

1 The great pronouncement of Jesus found in full in the cure of the man with the withered arm and repeated in abbreviated form in the healing of the man with dropsy:

> Is it permitted to do good or to do evil on the Sabbath, to save life or to destroy it (*Mark 3:4; Luke 14:3*).

'To do good' and 'to save life' are both seen as the actions of God. The well-known phrase 'Jesus went about doing good' does not mean that Jesus was just a good man doing good deeds. It means that he was acting as the Messiah, for 'to do good' is a Messianic action. As Messiah, Jesus is above the Jewish Law (Mark 2:28).

2 The cure of the enfeebled woman and the healing of the man with dropsy both contain the clearest evidence against the taking of the Sabbath law too far. If an animal can be looked after or rescued on the Sabbath day, then it seems somewhat strange that a person in need could not be helped. Jesus pointed out that taking the law this far was not in the interests of people.

Mark has grouped these five conflict stories at the beginning of his Gospel in order to show that Jesus is opposed to the religious authorities from the outset. Each story contains a different claim by Jesus that set himself against the religious leaders and pointed to the new way of Christianity:

1 ... the Son of Man has the right on earth to forgive sins (*Mark 2:10*).

2 I did not come to invite virtuous people, but sinners (*Mark 2:17*).

3 Can you expect the bridegroom's friends to fast while the bridegroom is with them? (*Mark 2:19*).

4 ... the Son of Man is sovereign even over the Sabbath (*Mark 2:28*).

5 Is it permitted to do good or to do evil on the Sabbath; to save life or to kill? (*Mark 3:4*).

The key to all five claims is the authority of Jesus. Jesus can claim these things because of who he is:

1 He has the authority of God to forgive sins.
2 He has come to bring sinners back to God.
3 His presence among people is one of joy like a bridegroom at a wedding.
4 He is not restricted by the limitations of the Law, especially if he can 'do good' and 'save life'.

Interpretation for today

Sometimes today Christianity is misunderstood. Some people think of Christians as being like the Pharisees. They think Christians live by a strict set of rules and regulations. They see the Church as something negative; a group of Christians whose main cry is 'You must not do this and you must not do that.' They also accuse Christians of pretending to be morally superior and of taking great delight in their virtue.

Many Christians would admit freely that, at times, the Church does give this impression, but they would stress that it is a false impression and has little to do with what Christianity is all about.

Christians believe that the message of Jesus is one of reconciliation. It is a joyful message in which every individual is of value to God and to each other. It is a positive message in which the keeping of the moral commandments of behaviour become a vital part of the relationship with God and with each other. This relationship is based on love. It is not a relationship in which rules are kept because of either fear or the belief that such action will bring some reward.

The message of the Nature miracles for today

Some Christians claim that the Nature miracles are simple stories of what Jesus did and should be accepted as such.

Some try to explain the miracles away and say that they did not happen.

Other Christians would say that, while the stories may be based on some happening in the life of Jesus, the importance of the Nature miracles is that they teach people crucial matters of faith in Jesus.

- *Jesus acts with the authority and power of God (The Calming of the Storm).*
- *The Christian should remember that Jesus will not desert his modern-day disciples who may be called on to suffer for their faith (The Calming of the Storm).*
- *Most Christians today believe that Jesus 'feeds' his people in the Eucharistic celebration (The feeding of the 5000).*

- *All Christians today believe Jesus is the Son of God, and that when he was conducting his ministry on earth, even though he was fully human, he was also divine. He did the things only God can do (The Walking on the Water).*

The message of these miracles is a simple one. Most Christians believe that the needs of an individual person are more important than any slavish observance of religious law. Just as in Jesus' time, concern for the sick, underprivileged, outcast and those without rights or oppressed should be unquestionable.

The Response of the Sinner and Interpretations for Today

In the House of Simon the Pharisee (Luke 7:36–50)

The Story

Jesus was invited to dinner at the house of Simon the Pharisee (see also Luke 11:37; 14:1).

Simon behaved in a rather superior way and did not offer Jesus the usual courtesies given to a guest. He had not provided water to wash the feet and had not given him the traditional greeting of a kiss (Luke 7:44–45). While they were eating, a woman who had a bad name crept into the room and knelt at the feet of Jesus. She was crying and began to anoint Jesus' feet with myrrh which she had brought with her. Simon criticised Jesus for allowing such an immoral woman to touch him. The criticism was not made out loud but Jesus sensed what Simon was thinking.

In reply Jesus told the parable of the two debtors, a simple story about two men, one of whom owed a lot of money and the other a little. They were both excused their debts by the creditor.

Which will love him more? (*Luke 7:42*).

Meaning

The meaning of the story can be summarised as follows:

(a) The greater the amount of forgiveness, the more grateful is the person forgiven (Luke 7:47).

(b) Simon had little reason to be grateful or even appreciative of Jesus because he did not have a sense of wrong. He considered himself to be superior:

> ... where little has been forgiven, little love is shown (*Luke 7:47*).

The foundation stone of love is forgiveness because this can bring people together.

(c) Jesus commented on the woman's actions:

> ... I tell you, her great love proves that her many sins have been forgiven (*Luke 7:47*).

There is no mention of the occasion when this forgiveness had taken place. Perhaps the woman had already met Jesus previously, had changed her immoral life, in so doing had realised that her sins had been forgiven and was now showing gratitude for this.

(d) Jesus confirmed this forgiveness:

> Your sins are forgiven (*Luke 7:48*).

Immediately this was questioned by the other guests as, according to the Jews, only God had the authority to forgive sins. Jesus ignored their murmurings. He was more concerned with the woman:

> Your faith has saved you; go in peace (*Luke 7:50*).

Interpretation for today

Christians today believe that Jesus has the authority to forgive sins. They would also claim that such forgiveness is important in their lives for, without the forgiveness of God and each other, it is seen as impossible to be reconciled with God.

Some Christians, notably those belonging to the Roman Catholic tradition, receive the Sacrament of Reconciliation, popularly called 'Confession'. Within this sacrament, a person may, through the intermediary of the priest, confess sins to God, and receive God's absolution. Other Churches do not see the need for such a sacramental structure and urge their people to ask God directly for the forgiveness of sins.

Zacchaeus (Luke 19:1–10)

The Story

Zacchaeus was a tax-collector and was very unpopular with the Jews, not only because he worked for the Romans but also because he was very rich through cheating people, as he himself admitted (Luke 19:8).

This little man wanted to see Jesus and climbed a sycamore tree to get a better view. Jesus had probably been told about Zacchaeus and so was able to call him by name. He told him that he wanted to stay with him. This action received the usual disapproval although, for once, not from the Jewish leaders but from the crowd in general. This shows the extent to which Zacchaeus was disliked.

Zacchaeus made a public confession of his past and declared he was ready to make amends. He volunteered to do two things:

1 to give half his property to charity;
2 to repay fourfould those he had cheated.

After this, no one could call Zacchaeus a sinner again. He was restored to his rightful place in the Jewish community, for he was a 'son of Abraham' (Luke 19:9):

> Salvation has come to this house today! (*Luke 19:9*).

Meaning

The important truth about this story is not that Zacchaeus had a change of heart as though he had suddenly decided that the way back to God was through good works of charity. Zacchaeus became reconciled to God because Jesus, instead of ignoring him or treating him like an outcast, had deliberately gone out of his way to meet and befriend him.

Interpretation for today

Christians believe that when a person meets Jesus they can turn their back on the past and return to a life with God. They believe this meeting with Jesus can happen in many ways: through the love of friends or family; through other human relationships; through the Church; through the scriptures – to name but some of the ways.

They also believe that, like Zacchaeus, many people who have come back to God desire to make amends for their past. This need not follow the pattern laid down by Zacchaeus but can be something as simple as turning the back on the past and seeking reconciliation with God and other people.

Study Skills

Knowledge

1 Which disciples were brothers?
2 What was the occupation of Levi?
3 What does the nickname 'Peter' mean?
4 What did Peter say in answer to the question, 'Who do you say I am?'?
5 What did Jesus say to the paralysed man that so angered the Pharisees?
6 What did Jesus say to the Scribes of the Pharisees' party when they

criticised him for eating with sinners and tax-collectos in Levi's house?
7. How did the disciples break the Sabbath law when they were walking through the cornfields?
8. What did Jesus say when he was criticised for healing a man with the withered hand on the Sabbath?
9. Whose house was Jesus in when he was anointed by the sinful woman?
10. Why did the woman anoint Jesus?
11. What was the occupation of Zacchaeus?
12. Why did Jesus want to stay with Zacchaeus?

Understanding

13. Why do you think the Pharisees criticised Jesus for allowing his disciples to pluck ears of corn on the Sabbath? Give reasons for your answer.
14. Jesus said that the disciple must 'leave self behind; he must take up his cross, and come with me'. What do you understand Jesus to mean by these words?

Evaluation

15. Why do you think that people such as the sinful woman and Zacchaeus responded to Jesus?
16. Choose one occasion when Jesus disagreed with the Pharisees. Give both sides of the argument and state which side you agree with and why.
17. What do you understand by the word 'vocation'? Do you think that it is true to say that all Christians have a vocation? If so, in what ways can vocation be expressed today?

Examination Practice

Describe what happened when Jesus went for a meal at the house of Simon the Pharisee. (6)
Name one other occasion when Jesus forgave sins. (2)
Why do you think Jesus opposed the Pharisees? (6)
Does the difference in Jesus' and the Pharisees' attitudes to religion have any relevance for Christians today? (6)

Practical Work

- Find out all you can about the Pharisees and Scribes. Present this information on large sheets of paper for display. Underline all the points on which Jesus came into conflict with the Pharisees and Scribes. Produce a section of the display in which the teaching of Jesus is shown.
- Write an account about any Christian who lost his or her life through being a disciple of Jesus.

CHAPTER

6 The Suffering and Death of Jesus

The suffering and death of Jesus is such an important part of the story of Jesus that each of the Gospel writers devotes a major part of his Gospel to it: Matthew, seven chapters; Luke, five chapters; and Mark, one-third of his Gospel, five chapters. Considerable time must be given to its study. There are three main areas of study to be covered:

– The narrative of Holy Week
– What the Evangelists believe about the death of Jesus
– What the death of Jesus means for Christians today

The Narrative of Holy Week

Mark has arranged the events of the last days of Jesus into a one-week period. This is, in all probability, a condensed reconstruction as the events in Jerusalem may well have lasted longer than a single week. Luke, even though his order of material is basically the same as Mark, tries to give the impression that it was a longer period of time (see Luke 19:47; 20:1; 21:38; 22:1, 7). Matthew follows Mark very closely although he inserts, in blocks, some of his own material into the week (for example, Matt. 25:1–46).

Scholars believe the Passion narrative was the earliest continuous account of events in the life of Jesus to take a fixed form. It may well be that Mark made the events fit a single week because the Church was already celebrating a 'Holy Week', thereby giving a structure to the early Christian celebrations.

The events of the last week can be tabulated. The order given in the table below follows that of Mark. References to the parallel passages in Matthew and Luke are given in brackets. (Where passages in Luke are recorded outside of the Holy Week narrative, the references are marked with an asterisk.)

SUNDAY (6.00 pm Sat – 6.00 pm Sun)

The entry into Jerusalem .... Mark 11:1–11
(Matt. 21:1–9; Luke 19:28–38)

MONDAY (6.00 pm Sun – 6.00 pm Mon)

The cursing of the fig tree .... Mark 11:12–14
(Matt. 21:18–19)
The cleansing of the Temple .... Mark 11:15–19
(Matt. 21:10–17; Luke 19:45–48)

TUESDAY (6.00 pm Mon – 6.00 pm Tues)

The meaning of the withered fig tree .... Mark 11:20–26
(Matt. 21:20–22)
The question of authority .... Mark 11:27–33
(Matt. 21:23–27; Luke 20:1–8)
The Parable of the Tenants .... Mark 12:1–12
(Matt. 21:33–46; Luke 20:9–19)
The question of paying taxes to Caesar .... Mark 12:13–17
(Matt. 22:15–22; Luke 20:20–26)
The question about resurrection .... Mark 12:18–27
(Matt. 22:23–33; Luke 20:27–40)
The question about the greatest commandment .... Mark 12:28–34
(Matt. 22:34–40; Luke 10:25–28*)

Jesus teaches in the Temple

  (1) David's son .... Mark 12:35–37
(Matt. 22:41–46; Luke 20:41–44)
  (2) Against the Scribes .... Mark 12:38–40
(Matt. 23:1–36; Luke 20:45–47)
  (3) The widow's coins .... Mark 12:41–44
(Luke 21:1–4)

WEDNESDAY (6.00 pm Tues – 6.00 pm Wed)

The plot against Jesus .... Mark 14:1–2
(Matt. 26:1–5; Luke 22:1–2)
The anointing at Bethany .... Mark 14:3–9
(Matt. 26:6–13; Luke 7:36–50*)
Judas plans his betrayal .... Mark 14:10–11
(Matt. 26:14–16; Luke 22:3–6)

THURSDAY (6.00 pm Wed – 6.00 pm Thurs)

Preparations for the Passover .... Mark 14:12–16
(Matt. 26:17–19; Luke 22:7–13)

FRIDAY (6.00 pm Thurs – 6.00 pm Fri)

The Last Supper

   (1) The treachery of Judas foretold .... Mark 14:17–21
                                        (Matt. 26:20–25; Luke 22:21–23)
   (2) The institution of the Eucharist .... Mark 14:22–25
                                        (Matt. 26:26–29; Luke 22:15–20)
   (3) Peter's denial foretold .... Mark 14:26–31
                                        (Matt. 26:30–35; Luke 22:31–34)

The Garden of Gethsemane .... Mark 14:32–42
                                        (Matt. 26:36–46; Luke 22:40–46)
The arrest of Jesus .... Mark 14:43–52
                                        (Matt. 26:47–56; Luke 22:47–53)
The trial before the Sanhedrin .... Mark 14:53–65
                                        (Matt. 26:57–68; Luke 22:66–71)
Peter's denial .... Mark 14:66–72
                                        (Matt. 26:69–75; Luke 22:54–62)
The trial before Pilate .... Mark 15:1–15
                                    (Matt. 27:1–26; Luke 23:1–5, 17–25)
The mocking of Jesus .... Mark 15:16–20
                                        (Matt. 27:27–31)

The crucifixion

   (1) The way of the cross .... Mark 15:21–22
                                        (Matt. 27:32; Luke 23:26–32)
   (2) The crucifixion .... Mark 15:23–32
                                        (Matt. 27:33–44; Luke 23:33–43)
   (3) The death on the cross .... Mark 15:33–39
                                        (Matt. 27:45–54; Luke 23:44–48)
   (4) The women watch at the crucifixion .... Mark 15:40–41
                                        (Matt. 27:55–56; Luke 23:49)

The burial .... Mark 15:42–47
                                        (Matt. 27:57–61; Luke 23:50–56)

SATURDAY (6.00 pm Fri – 6.00 pm Sat)

The Sabbath

SUNDAY (6.00 pm Sat – 6.00 pm Sun)

The empty tomb .... Mark 16:1–8
                                        (Matt. 28:1–10; Luke 24:1–11)

In studying the narrative of the last week of Jesus, the following notes are based on Mark's text. Where there is a need to comment on any major alternative offered by Matthew or Luke, either a separate note is given or comments are incorporated in the main discussion of the text.

Sunday (6.00 pm Sat – 6.00 pm Sun)

The Entry into Jerusalem (Mark 11:1–11; Matt. 21:1–9; Luke 19:28–38)

There are two possible ways to interpret this story of 'Palm Sunday'.

The first is to see the story as one of Messianic action. The claim of Jesus to be the Messiah was made public when Jesus rode the donkey into Jerusalem. This action emphasised that Jesus was a peaceful Messiah and not a military leader. Mark quotes from Psalms 118:26:

> Blessings on him who comes in the name of the Lord! (*Mark 11:10*).

Mark sees the Messiahship of Jesus in

> ... the coming kingdom of our father David (*Mark 11:10*).

Mark indicates that the crowd at this stage recognised Jesus as Messiah but by the end of the week they had changed their minds and were calling for his execution.

The second way to interpret the story carries little Messianic significance at all. It has been suggested that Jesus rode into Jerusalem at the time of the Feast of Dedication, which came just before the Passover. This feast celebrated the dedication of the Temple and, as part of the celebration, branches and palms were waved and Psalm 118 chanted. It may be that the crowd did not see any Messianic meaning in Jesus' actions.

(*Matthew*: Matthew wishes to emphasise the Messianic role of Jesus and includes in his account a quotation from the prophet Zechariah. The action of Jesus is seen as fulfilling Messianic prophecy:

'... see, your King is coming to you,
his cause won, his victory gained,
humble and mounted on an ass,
on a foal, the young of a she-ass' (Zechariah 9:9).)

(*Luke*: Luke adds to the quotation from Psalm 118, used by Mark, the words:

Peace in heaven, glory in the highest heaven! (*Luke 19:38*).

These words are very similar to those found in the song of the angel choir at the birth of Jesus, when the Angel of the Lord announces the birth of the Messiah to the shepherds (Luke 2:11–14).)

Monday (6.00 pm Sun – 6.00 pm Mon)

The Cursing of the Fig Tree (Mark 11:12–14; Matt. 21:18–19)

This is a difficult story to understand because Jesus seems to be acting out of character. Mark himself states that it would have been remarkable for Jesus to have found fruit on the tree for it was not even the proper season for fruit. It has been suggested that the story was originally a parable aimed at the Pharisees, which is, in Mark, out of context. (This is how the story is recorded in Luke 13:6–9, where the fig tree stood for the self-righteous people, such as the Pharisees, who made a great show of their religion but produced few results. They are condemned. Soon it would be too late and Jerusalem, the centre of their religion, would be destroyed. This was to happen in 70 AD.)

The Cleansing of the Temple (Mark 11:15–19; Matt. 21:10–17; Luke 19:45–48)

In the prophecy of Malachi it says, 'Suddenly the Lord whom you seek will come to his Temple' (Malachi 3:1). It may be that this prophecy lies behind the account of the expulsion from the Temple of those who bought and sold.

Mark states that, after the cursing of the fig tree, Jesus went into the Temple and:

1. drove out those who bought and sold;
2. upset the tables of the money changers;
3. upset the chairs of those who sold the sacrificial pigeons;
4. stopped people carrying things through the Temple, using it as a short cut.

Traders in the Temple sold sacrifices to pilgrims coming to Jerusalem. These sacrifices could only be bought with special Temple money because foreign currency such as Roman coins, showing the heads of pagan rulers, could not be used inside the perimeter of the Temple. In addition, the suggestion has been made that the rates of exchange favoured the Temple and its priests. Using the Temple as a short cut was also forbidden by Jewish Law and yet the priests turned a blind eye to it because it brought more trade into the Temple.

When Jesus challenged this use of the Temple, he was really challenging the authority of the priests. The words of Jesus are a combination of Isaiah (56:7) and Jeremiah (7:11):

> My house shall be called a house of prayer for all the nations. But you have made it a robbers' cave (*Mark 11:17*).

It is somewhat surprising that Jesus could get away with such drastic action. Mark, aware of the problem, records that the reaction of the chief priests and Scribes was to look for some way to get rid of Jesus, but that they could not do so at that moment because Jesus was popular with the people.

Tuesday (6.00 pm Mon – 6.00 pm Tues)

The Meaning of the Withered Fig Tree (Mark 11:20–26; Matt. 21:20–22)

Mark states that the next morning Jesus and his disciples walked passed the fig tree that had been cursed the previous day. Peter noticed that the tree had withered and died. Jesus uses the opportunity to teach the disciples the nature of faith. If they had sufficient faith, then anything was possible. The mountain may be cast into the sea. Faith plays a full part in the process of prayer. If a person prays believing that the prayer will be answered, then that person will receive an answer.

The Question of Authority (Mark 11:27–33; Matt. 21:23–27; Luke 20:1–8)

This is the first of a series of questions designed to trap Jesus into saying something that could lead to his arrest. The Jewish authorities had already decided to do away with him (Mark 11:18).

The first group to challenge Jesus were representatives of the Sanhedrin: Mark calls them the priests, Scribes and elders (Mark 11:27). It was quite natural for them to challenge Jesus, especially in view of his own challenge to their authority the previous day, when he ordered out of the Temple those who had permission to trade there (Mark 11:15–18).

The question they asked Jesus was a trap:

> Who gave you authority to act in this way? (*Mark 11:28*).

Whatever reply Jesus gave would have placed him in danger. If he had said his authority came from God, he would have faced a charge of blasphemy. If he had said he was acting under his own authority, he would have laid himself open to ridicule.

Jesus refused to answer the question. Instead, he asked a question in return:

> The baptism of John: was it from God or from men? (*Mark 11:30*).

John had called the people to repent and had baptised those who had responded. The questioners were now placed in the same difficulty as Jesus had been in. If they said John was acting as a man, they would make the people angry because they considered John to be a prophet. If they said John was a prophet and thereby received his authority from God, they would be criticised for not listening to him. In the end they refused to answer, which allowed Jesus to refuse to answer as well.

It would be wrong to consider that Jesus had simply evaded the question. He is, in one sense, saying that his own authority came from God. After all, he had been baptised by John and his authority stemmed from that moment:

> Thou art my Son, my beloved; on thee my favour rests (*Mark 1:11*).

The Parable of the Tenants (Mark 12:1–12; Matt. 21:33–46; Luke 20:9–19)

This is one of the best examples of allegory in the Gospels. The parable is based on Isaiah 5:1–7 where there is an Old Testament 'parable' about a vineyard that yielded only wild grapes. This signified the faithlessness of Israel.

The allegory has obviously been developed, in the period of the early Church, to show what is known as *salvation history*. Salvation history is the story of God and his people and how God, since creation, has attempted to reconcile them to himself. The allegory is easily understood using the following key:

the owner of the vineyard	= God
the vineyard	= Israel
the tenants	= Jewish leaders
the servants	= the prophets
the son	= Jesus
the killing of the son	= the crucifixion
others	= Gentiles
the stone	= the resurrection of Jesus

Verses 10–11 are not part of the original story; they record a saying used by the early Church to indicate the resurrection. Jesus, rejected and put to death by the Jewish leaders, rises to become the keystone of the new faith of Christianity. The saying has been included to

complete the story of salvation history because to end with the killing of the son would have been incomplete.

Jesus' audience, however, would not have recognised the 'son' as Jesus because they would not have realised that he was going to die. There must, therefore, have been another meaning of the parable before it was developed into an allegory.

The parable is a true to life description of a Galilean peasant's attitude towards the foreign landlords of which there were many. The parable may refer to the fact that in Jesus' time the Zealots (this was a name given to nationalists) were stirring up the peasants to revolt against such landlords.

The fact that the owner of the vineyard lives abroad is the key to understanding the parable. The tenants take liberties with the messengers because they know that the owner is far away. The son's arrival makes the tenants think that the owner is dead and that the son has come to claim his inheritance. According to Jewish Law, if the vineyard became ownerless then it became the property of the tenants. So they kill the son to acquire the vineyard.

Perhaps, in this parable, Jesus is criticising the Jewish leaders who, in their self-righteousness, had not listened to God. They rejected both God and his messengers. So the vineyard is given to others. Perhaps Jesus meant by this the 'outcasts' of Jewish society, although it is equally possible that he meant that God's message – the kingdom – was for everyone, regardless of race.

The process of the development from parable to allegory can be clearly seen when a comparison is made of the three accounts in the Synoptic Gospels.

	Mark	**Matthew**	**Luke**
Setting	Based on allegory found in Isaiah.	Based on allegory found in Isaiah.	Simple beginning to parable.
Tenants	Three separate servants, then a group (this shows some degree of allegorisation).	Two groups, the second larger than the first (this is the most developed allegorically, showing the major and minor prophets).	Three separate servants (this is most like a parable).
Outcome	The son is killed and then thrown out of the vineyard.	The son is killed and then thrown out of the vineyard.	The son is taken out of the vineyard and then killed (this shows some degree of allegorisation as Jesus was taken out of the city to be crucified).

The Question of Paying Taxes to Caesar (Mark 12:13–17; Matt 22:15–22; Luke 20:20–26)

The second question designed to trap Jesus follows a similar pattern to the first. This time Mark and Matthew say the question was asked by the Pharisee and Herodians, while Luke simply called them 'spies'. The question they asked was:

> Are we or are we not permitted to pay taxes to the Roman Emperor? (*Mark 12:14*).

Once again Jesus was faced with the problem of answering. If he had said 'Yes', he would have become unpopular with the people, who hated the tax. He would also have become even more unpopular than he already was with the Pharisees, who were bitterly opposed to the Roman occupation.

If he said said 'No', he would have been committing treason against Rome.

The tax was a poll-tax imposed by the Romans in 6 AD. It was extremely unpopular because it was a symbol of Roman rule. The Roman coins showed the head and inscription of the Emperor. They belonged to him and were used only by his authority.

Jesus called for a coin and asked whose head and inscription were engraved on it. When they said 'Caesar's' his comment was:

> Pay Caesar what is due to Caesar, and pay God what is due to God (*Mark 12:17*).

What Jesus meant by this answer was:

1 the Jews already recognised the Romans as the state authority;
2 they had a duty to recognise civil authority;
3 there was a further allegiance to God.

The Question about Resurrection (Mark 12:18–27; Matt. 22:23–33; Luke 20:27–40)

It is natural that the third test question of Holy Week should have been asked by the Sadducees. They did not believe in any form of resurrection yet they asked a question concerning this topic.

The question was based on an ancient Jewish law called the Leverite law (Deuteronomy 25:5–6). The purpose of the law, which was not widely practised by the time of Jesus, was to preserve both a family line and the inheritance of family possessions and property. The question asked of Jesus was overemphasised by the Sadducees to the point of being absurd.

There were seven brothers. The eldest married but died childless.

The second, third, fourth and so on each, in turn, married the widow and died childless. Finally, the woman herself died. Whose wife will she be at the resurrection?

The reply of Jesus is in two distinct parts:

(a) **At the resurrection people do not marry**. They will be like angels. What Jesus is saying is that there is no need for marriage at the resurrection. Marriage is an earthly institution that ends at death.

(b) **There is a resurrection**. Jesus claimed that such a truth is implied in the Scriptures. When God appeared to Moses at the time of the burning bush, Moses was told,

> I am the God of Abraham, the God of Isaac and the God of Jacob (*Mark 12:26*).

These three Jewish leaders were long since dead but God spoke as though they were still alive. He said 'I am' their God not 'I was' their God. This indicates that they are still alive:

> God is not God of the dead but of the living (*Mark 12:27*).

The Question about the Greatest Commandment (Mark 12:28–34; Matt. 22:34–40; Luke 10:25–28)*

The fourth question was asked by a Scribe or lawyer. The Scribes were all Doctors of the Law. In the written law there were some 613 different commandments. Technically, they were all equally important but debates often took place as to their relative importance. Jesus was asked his opinion. Which commandment did he consider to be the greatest?

In reply Jesus quoted the daily prayer of the Jews called the Shema (Deuteronomy 6:4–5):

> Hear, O Israel: the Lord our God is the only Lord; love the Lord your God with all your heart, with all your soul, with all your mind. (*Mark 12:29–30*).

The second part of Jesus' answer was a quotation from the book of Leviticus (19:18):

> Love your neighbour as yourself (*Mark 12:31*).

In Leviticus 'neighbour' meant 'Israelite' or 'fellow-countryman'. It is probable that Jesus extended this to mean anyone of any race.

For once, the Scribe does not oppose Jesus. In Mark's Gospel he goes on to commend Jesus. The love of God and of one's neighbour is more valuable than sacrifice. In turn, again only in Mark, Jesus complimented the Scribe for his great insight, saying that he was not far from the kingdom of God.

(*Luke*: Luke does not record this story in Holy Week but uses a form of it earlier in his Gospel. He treats the story as an introduction to the Parable of the Good Samaritan (see chapter 3).)

Jesus Teaches in the Temple

(a) **David's son** (Mark 12:35–37; Matt. 22:41–46; Luke 20:41–44). Having endured this series of questions designed to trap him, Jesus returned the compliment with a question directed against the Scribes.

He quoted a passage from the Psalms in which God speaks to the Messiah and sets him at his right hand until all enemies have been overcome. The writer of the Psalms was believed to be King David. So Jesus asked the question: How can the Messiah be the son of David if David refers to him as Lord?

There are two ways of interpreting this comment of Jesus. The first is to look upon it as a simple riddle to which the Scribes seemingly had no answer. The second is to understand that Jesus is arguing that the Messiah is not a descendant of David. At first, such an interpretation seems impossible as all the Scriptures place the Messiah in the line of David. Perhaps Jesus is refuting the popular idea of Messiah, which was that a descendant of David would come as a nationalistic leader, drive the Romans out and restore the kingdom of Israel.

(b) **Against the Scribes** (Mark 12:38–40; Matt. 23:1–36; Luke 20:45–47). The Scribes loved to receive the praise of ordinary people. They enjoyed the special places reserved for them in the synagogues which were in full view of the congregation. They enjoyed the greetings of people in the street and they loved places of honour at banquets. They made a great show of prayers but treated people wrongly. Jesus said they would receive a severe sentence for their hypocrisy.

(c) **The widow's coins** (Mark12:41–44; Luke 21:1–4). In stark contrast to the attitude of the Scribes and Pharisees, Jesus pointed to a poor widow who had just come into the Temple and placed two small coins into the offertory box. The box was called the treasury and was simply a chest, shaped like a trumpet, into which people put their offerings. Jesus praised the widow's small offering which was all she had. The much larger offerings of the rich were, in comparison to their wealth, small offerings indeed.

Wednesday (6.00 pm Tues – 6.00 pm Wed)

The Plot Against Jesus (Mark 14:1–2; Matt. 26:1–5; Luke 22:1–2)

The story of the Passion continues with the statement by the chief priests and Scribes that they were seeking to arrest Jesus and put him to death. They decided, however, that they could not do this during the coming festival of Passover because Jesus was still popular among the people and they did not want to cause unrest.

It is possible to pinpoint the time of this decision of the Jewish leaders if Mark's account is followed. He records:

> ... the festival of Passover and Unleavened Bread was only two days off *(Mark 14:1).*

(*Luke and Matthew*: Luke, who does not follow Mark's timing to the letter, merely says that the two festivals were drawing near (Luke 22:1). Matthew follows Mark with regard to the timing but omits the reference to the festival of Unleavened Bread.)

FESTIVAL OF UNLEAVENED BREAD

- Originally this was a separate feast to Passover.
- By the time of Jesus the two festivals were celebrated at the same time.
- Yeast was only used once a year.
- A piece of dough was kept back after using the yeast and this is called leaven.
- This leaven was added the next time baking bread was done.
- This process was then repeated throughout the year until the festival.
- The main symbol of the feast was the use of *unleavened* bread (that is bread without the leaven added) for a whole week.
- This symbolised a break with the past and all its sin and the making of a fresh start.

The Anointing at Bethany (Mark 14:3–9; Matt. 26:6–13; Luke 7:36–50*)

The anointing at Bethany is recorded by Mark and Matthew. There is no major difference between the two accounts. The anointing takes place in the house of Simon the leper, which was in Bethany.

The story is highly symbolic as the action of anointing is Messianic. The word 'Messiah' means 'anointed one'. It should be noted that:

1. Kings were anointed at their crowning as the regent of God on earth.
2. On taking office priests were anointed as those responsible in leading the worship of God.
3. Bodies were anointed after death for burial. Jesus claimed that the woman anointed him in readiness for death.
4. Mark is using this story to show that Jesus is the anointed one, and that, as Messiah, he was about to suffer and die.

(*Luke*: Luke's account of the anointing of Jesus takes place much earlier in the Gospel and carries a different meaning (see chapter 5).)

Judas Plans his Betrayal (Mark 14:10–11; Matt. 26:14–16; Luke 22:3–6)

The story of Judas is an excellent example of how traditions developed in the period of the early Church. If Mark's Gospel is read first, then Matthew's, Luke's and even John's, then a pattern of development as to the motive of Judas in betraying Jesus is clearly shown. Even today suggestions are still being made as to Judas' motive.

Mark: Judas decided to betray Jesus and told the chief priest that he would lead them to Jesus in order that they could arrest him in secret. This would avoid causing trouble with the people (Mark 14:2). In return for this information the chief priests promised to give him money.

Matthew: Matthew makes Judas out to be a greedy man who asked for money. The chief priests promised to give him thirty pieces of silver which, according to the Old Testament, was the price of a slave.

Luke and John: Both Luke and John claim that the Devil entered into Judas. John goes further and not only calls Judas a thief but also says that he was chosen by God to perform this evil deed.

The interpretation of the betrayal of Judas today

It has been suggested that the real reason Judas betrayed Jesus was that he wanted him to be a popular Messiah who would drive out the Romans. He was either trying to force Jesus' hand to make him fight or he had become so disappointed in Jesus that he acted out of bitterness.

What does the betrayal of Judas really mean? There are two views. The first is the most popular. The betrayal was leading the Temple police to Jesus. After all, before Jesus could be arrested he had to be found. Judas knew where he would be. The second view is that Judas told the chief priests that Jesus had claimed to be some sort of Messiah; perhaps one who would lead a rebellion against the Romans. This is possible as it is obvious in Mark's Gospel especially that the disciples did not really understand what the Messiahship of Jesus meant.

Study Skills

Knowledge

1. What instructions did Jesus give when he sent his disciples to fetch the colt?
2. How did the Jewish leaders react to the cleansing of the Temple?
3. How did the owner prepare the vineyard in the Parable of the Tenants?
4. How is the resurrection included in the parable?
5. What did Jesus say when he was asked if it was permitted to pay taxes to Caesar?
6. What was the Leverite law?
7. Which commandment did Jesus consider to be the greatest?
8. What was the feast of Unleavened Bread?
9. In which village, according to both Matthew and Mark, did the anointing of Jesus take place?
10. Who decided to betray Jesus?

Understanding

11. What do you think the story of Jesus' entry into Jerusalem means?
12. Explain the meaning of the Parable of the Tenants.

Evaluation

13. 'Judas' betrayal is one in which most Christians share.' Do you agree with this statement? Give reasons for your answer.

Thursday (6.00 pm Wed – 6.00 pm Thurs)

Preparations for the Passover (Mark 14:12–16; Matt. 26:17–19; Luke 22:7–13)

All three Synoptic Gospels make it clear which day it is. It is Thursday. The disciples (Luke names Peter and John) were sent, by prearranged plan, to prepare a room in Jerusalem for the evening's celebration of the Passover.

THE FESTIVAL OF PASSOVER

The festival of Passover celebrated the Exodus, the greatest event in Jewish history, when Moses, sent by God, led the children of Israel out of captivity from Egypt. On the night of their escape, Moses had commanded the Jews to sacrifice a lamb and smear the blood on the doorposts of their homes as a sign that they were to be 'passed over' by the Angel of Death, who was to bring death to the first born of every Egyptian family. They were to eat the lamb with unleavened bread and bitter herbs (Exodus 12:8–11). The exodus became the symbol of the 'passing over' from slavery to freedom. It is celebrated each year by the Jews.

The celebration meal is divided into four main sections:

1 Introduction

(a) The meal begins with a blessing of the first cup of wine by the eldest male present (called the paterfamilias). The cup is drunk as a symbol of joy at being able to celebrate the meal once again.
(b) A dish of bitter herbs is served. This reminds the company of their bitter captivity in Egypt.

2 The Passover celebration

(a) The story of the Passover is told by the paterfamilias in response to the question of the youngest member present: 'What is the meaning of this night?'
(b) This general outline story of the first Passover is called the *Haggadah*, after which the first part of the special Psalms for Passover are sung, known as the *Hallel Psalms* (Psalms 112–13).
(c) This is followed by the drinking of the second cup of wine, the 'Hallel cup'.

3 The Passover meal

(a) The main meal begins with words of blessing over the unleavened bread, which symbolises the urgency of the first Passover (Exodus 12:11). The words of this blessing would most probably be:

'Praise to you Lord, King of the universe
who causes bread to come from the earth.'

(b) The eating of the lamb, bread and the rest of the bitter herbs now takes place.

(c) The meal ends with the blessing and drinking of the third cup. The words of blessing are similar to those used over the bread:

'Praise to you, Lord, King of the universe
who feeds the world with goodness . . .'

4 Conclusion

(a) The meal concludes with the singing of the second part of the Hallel Psalms (Psalms 114–18).
(b) After this, the final act is the sharing of the fourth cup of wine.

WAS THE LAST SUPPER A PASSOVER MEAL?

There has always been a considerable dispute as to whether the Last Supper was a Passover meal. It has been argued that Jesus could not have been executed on Passover day because:

- the priests would not have held a trial on a feast day;
- execution on a feast day was impossible in Jewish Law.

Scholars who hold this view use three further pieces of information to support it:

1 The food eaten at Passover (e.g. roasted lamb, bitter herbs, unleavened bread) is not mentioned in the accounts.
2 The Haggadah is not mentioned.
3 Most important of all, John's Gospel claims that the Passover that year was on the Sabbath. Jesus was therefore, according to John, dead and buried before the Passover day began. The Last Supper cannot have been a Passover meal.

In contrast to this there is no doubt that all three synoptic writers intend their readers to understand the meal as that of the Passover. There are some striking similarities between the accounts of the Last Supper and the Passover meal.

1. There was a dish before the main meal (could this refer to the bitter herbs?) (Mark 14:20; Matt. 26:23).
2. Words were spoken over the bread and wine. This followed the pattern of the Passover meal when the paterfamilias had to explain the meaning of the food and wine (Mark 14:22–25; Matt. 26:26–29; Luke 22:19–20).
3. The bread was blessed and broken during the meal. This was rare in Jewish custom but it was demanded in the Passover celebration (Mark 14:22; Matt. 26:26; Luke 22:19).
4. Red wine was used. This was another regulation of the Passover celebration (Mark 14:24; Matt. 26:28; Luke 22:20).
5. Hymns (Psalms) were sung after the meal. This was another regulation of the Passover celebration (Mark 14:26; Matt. 26:30).

There is a solution to conflicting views about the Last Supper. At that time there was a dispute between the Pharisees and Sadducees as to when the festival should begin. The Pharisees held the meal one day before the official date. Jesus could have been following the custom of the Pharisees by celebrating Passover on the Thursday evening. John, in his Gospel, seems to be following the date set by the Sadducees and is therefore saying that Passover day was on the Sabbath, the day after the crucifixion.

Friday (6.00 pm Thurs – 6.00 pm Fri)

The Last Supper

(a) **The treachery of Judas foretold** (Mark 14:17–21; Matt. 26:20–25; Luke 22:21–23). See the notes on Mark 14:10–11; Matt. 26:14–16; Luke 22:3–6 (page 102).

(b) **The institution of the Eucharist** (Mark 14:22–25; Matt. 26:26–29; Luke 22:15–20). The accounts of the institution of the Eucharist are very important to Christians. They are central to the understanding of Christianity.

There are four accounts of the words of institution in the New Testament. It is obvious, however, that they come from two different traditions. Luke, following Paul's account in the first letter to the Corinthians, is probably the earliest tradition available. Mark and Matthew follow the other. A comparison between the accounts shows great similarity of thought between them.

1. The account of Paul and Luke
   (Words in *italics* are found only in Paul. Words in **bold** are found only in Luke.)

   This is my body, which is for you, do this as a memorial of me ... This cup, **poured out for you**, is the new covenant sealed by my blood. *Whenever you drink it, do this as a memorial of me* (1 Corinthians 11:24–25; Luke 22:19–20).

2. The accounts of Mark and Matthew
   (Words in *italics* are found only in Mark. Words in **bold** are found only in Matthew.)

   Take this **and eat**; this is my body ... **Drink from it all of you**. This is my blood, the blood of the covenant, shed for many **for the forgiveness of sins**. I tell you this: never again shall I drink from the fruit of the vine until that day when I drink it new **with you** in the kingdom *of God* (**of my Father**) (Mark 14:22–25; Matt. 26:26–29).

The importance of the Eucharistic words for Christians today

Most Christians would claim that the celebration of the Eucharist is one of the most important moments within Christianity, both in its beginnings at the Last Supper and in the life of the Church today.

The words of institution are the language of sacrifice; the breaking of the bread and the pouring of the wine symbolise the death of Jesus. Christians believe that through the death of Jesus a new relationship is made between God and his people, called the covenant. *In this relationship God forgives his people their sin. This is made possible through the death and resurrection of Jesus. These aspects of belief are at the very heart of the Eucharist itself.*

(c) **Peter's denial foretold** (Mark 14:26–31; Matt. 26:30–5; Luke 22:31–4). Immediately after the Last Supper, Jesus and his disciples went out to the Mount of Olives. Technically no one was allowed to leave the city on Passover night but by the time of Jesus there were so many pilgrims in the city that the rule was relaxed to include an area surrounding the city. The Mount of Olives was in that allowed area. It was at this time that Jesus told the disciples that they would all desert him.

Peter replied that he would never lose faith. Jesus forecast that before the cock crowed twice he would have denied any knowledge of Jesus three times. It was forbidden to keep cockerels within the city of Jerusalem so in all probability the 'cock crow' was an early morning time of the Roman day, perhaps a trumpet call.

(*Luke*: Luke records that the forecast of Peter's denial took place at the Last Supper itself. His account of the story comes from a different source to that of Mark. In Luke's account Jesus, in addition to forecasting the denial of Peter, also forecast that Peter would recover and become a source of strength to the other disciples. Peter's recovery is not found in the Gospel story but is one of the main themes of the early chapters of Luke's second book, the Acts of the Apostles.)

The Garden of Gethsemane (Mark 14:32–42; Matt. 26:36–46; Luke 22:40–46)

Jesus took Peter, James and John into the garden, the rest of the disciples having been told to wait for them. The three disciples were told to pray while Jesus went further into the garden to pray by himself. In Mark and Matthew's accounts Jesus returned three times and found the three asleep.

The story of the agony in the garden is the most descriptive picture of Jesus' humanity found in the Synoptic Gospels. Jesus felt despair and sorrow to such an extent that there is a mood of desperation in the story.

The despair and anguish felt by Jesus was so deep that it is difficult to translate the Greek words that Mark uses in his story. In Mark 14:33 the verbs are translated by the words 'horror' and 'dismay'. In Greek the first is much more than just horror. The following translations have been offered: 'suggestive of shuddering awe'; 'terrified surprise'; and 'amazement amounting to shock'. The second word carries the following meanings: 'distress that follows a great shock' and 'agitation'. The impact of both verbs together is overwhelming. They paint a picture of unbounded horror and suffering.

Jesus asked for the 'cup' to be taken away from him; the cup that stands for death:

> Abba, Father . . . all things are possible to thee; take this cup from me. Yet not what I will, but what thou wilt (*Mark 14:36*).

This prayer expresses the closest relationship between God and Jesus, as can be seen by the use of the word 'Abba'. Jesus was aware that suffering and death lay ahead of him and he was frightened. The story ends with the arrival of Judas.

(*Luke*: Luke's account of the agony of Jesus is different from that of the other two Evangelists:

1. Luke does not refer to the Garden of Gethsemane. He prefers the wider location of the Mount of Olives.
2. Jesus only goes to pray by himself once and not three times.
3. In Luke's story an angel came and comforted Jesus, as he prayed so earnestly that his sweat fell to the ground like drops of blood (Luke 22:43–44). These verses do not appear in all early manuscripts and there is some doubt as to whether they were originally part of Luke's Gospel.)

The Arrest of Jesus (Mark 14:43–52; Matt. 26:47–56; Luke 22:47–53)

Judas had arranged a signal with the men sent by the chief priests, Scribes and elders. The signal was one of great simplicity, a kiss. This was the common form of greeting. Judas came up to Jesus and kissed him. Jesus was arrested and in the struggle that followed the high priest's servant was injured. Mark and Matthew record:

> Then the disciples all deserted him and ran away (*Mark 14:50; Matt 26:56*).

At this point Mark alone includes the strange story of the young man who was also seized but who slipped out of his 'linen cloth' and escaped naked. It has been suggested that the young man was Mark himself.

(*Luke*: Once again Luke has the same story but with significant differences:

1. Luke states that Jesus refused to allow Judas to greet him with a kiss.
2. The servant of the high priest, who had lost an ear in the struggle, was healed by Jesus. It is doubtful if this detail is authentic. Jesus would hardly have been in a position to carry out this miracle of healing.
3. The disciples do not run away in Luke. Rather Luke emphasises that the whole event is the work of evil. He prefers to end with the words:

> ... this is your moment – the hour when darkness reigns (*Luke 22:53*).)

The Trial before the Sanhedrin (Mark 14:53–65; Matt. 26:57–68; Luke 22:66–71)

The Sanhedrin was the official court of Jewish justice (see chapter 1).

If Jesus was on trial then there are certain irregularities in the proceedings as recorded by Mark and Matthew:

1. The Sanhedrin did not meet at the high priest's house (Mark 14:53; Matt. 26:57).
2. Trials which involved the possible sentence of death were not allowed to be conducted at night (Mark 14:55; Matt. 26:59).
3. A verdict of guilty required the sentence to be delayed for twenty-four hours.
4. Witnesses were warned that if they gave false evidence they would suffer the same verdict as that given to the accused (Mark 14:56–7; Matt. 26:60–61).
5. At least two independent witnesses were needed to agree in evidence; if they did not agree, the trial was stopped and the accused found 'not guilty' (Mark 14:59).
6. No abuse of a prisoner was allowed during court proceedings (Mark 14:65; Matt. 26:67–68).

It may well be that the Jewish leaders did not consider the event to be a trial but more of an interrogation to see if there was enough evidence to take Jesus to the Roman Governor.

Throughout the trial Jesus remained silent. It was only when the high priest asked him the direct question:

> Are you the Messiah, the Son of the Blessed One? (the Son of God' in Matthew)

that Jesus spoke:

> I am ('you have said so' in Matthew) (*Mark 14:62; Matt. 26:64*).

This was enough to seal Jesus' fate. He was guilty of blasphemy and could now be taken to the Roman Governor with the recommendation that he suffer the death penalty.

(*Luke*: The account of the trial in Luke does not take place at night but in the morning. This avoids some of the difficulties. However, the trial as recorded by Luke is a confusing narrative that is built around three important titles of Jesus:

1. ... Are you the Messiah?

2. ... from now on, the Son of Man will be seated at the right hand of Almighty God;

3 **You are the Son of God, then?** (*Luke 22:67–70*).

It is impossible to see a logical pattern running through the narrative as Luke records it. The use of the title 'Son of Man' does not lead naturally to the thought that Jesus is claiming to be Son of God.)

Peter's Denial (Mark 14:66–72; Matt. 26:69–75; Luke 22:54–62)

Peter was accused three times, as he sat in the courtyard of the high priest's house, of being one of Jesus' men and three times he denied it. He had probably been seen with Jesus in and around Jerusalem. After the third time, the cock crew and Peter burst into tears.

The Trial before Pilate (Mark 15:1–15; Matt. 27:1–26; Luke 23:1–5, 17–25)

To a differing degree, all the Gospels portray Pontius Pilate, the Governor of Judaea from 26 to 36 AD, as a man who was reluctant to condemn Jesus and who would have preferred to set him free. This is understandable because the Gospels were written at a time when the Church had to exist in a Roman world.

In Mark and Matthew's Gospels, the charge brought to Pilate was that Jesus claimed to be 'the King of the Jews'. Pilate obviously did not consider this to be a threat to Roman authority and tried to have him released.

He offered to set Jesus free instead of a man called Barabbas, a nationalist who had led some minor revolt against the Romans. There is no historical evidence for the custom of releasing a prisoner at festival time, although such an amnesty was possible. The crowd shouted for the release of Barabbas and the death of Jesus. Pilate, in spite of declaring that Jesus had done no wrong, finally gave in to their demands and handed Jesus over to be crucified. The most probable reason for this unjust behaviour by the Roman Governor was that he feared some sort of riot breaking out in the capital city during the festival. Such trouble might well have resulted in Pilate being called back to Rome. This had happened by the time the Gospels were written.

Matthew: Matthew follows Mark's account very closely but includes two additions of his own:

1 Pilate's wife sent him a message begging him to have nothing to do with Jesus as she had experienced a bad dream because of him.
2 When Pilate realised that a riot was a distinct possibility, he

literally took water and washed his hands of the affair with the words:

> My hands are clean of this man's blood; see to that yourselves (*Matt. 27:25*).

This action is seen as absolving Pilate of guilt for the death of Jesus.

(*Luke*: Of the three Gospels, Luke's is the most dedicated in its wish to blame the Jews for the death of Jesus. Luke therefore goes out of his way to excuse the actions of Pilate:

1 The charges brought against Jesus were changed into political charges. This cast doubt on the integrity of the Jewish leaders. These political charges, such as opposing taxes to Caesar and inciting people to revolt, meant that Pilate could not simply ignore Jesus.
2 In spite of this, Luke stresses that Pilate tried hard, three times, to have Jesus released (Luke 23:4, 14, 22).
3 Luke even hints that the Romans did not carry out the execution of Jesus but that the responsibility was that of the Jews (Luke 23:25–26).)

The Mocking of Jesus (Mark 15:16–20; Matt. 27:27–31)

There is little evidence that the Romans used to flog their victims before crucifixion. The story about the scourging of Jesus may relate to the comment in Isaiah: '. . . by this scourging we are healed' (Isaiah 53:5).

After the scourging the soldiers mocked Jesus by dressing him up in purple, the royal colour, and giving him a crown of thorns and a reed for a sceptre. Then they made fun of him in mock homage, spitting at him and hitting him.

(*Luke*: The mock homage in Luke's account is carried out by Herod Antipas and not the Romans (Luke 23:6–12).)

The Crucifixion

(a) **The way of the cross** (Mark 15:21–22; Matt. 27:32; Luke 23:26–32). All three Snyoptic Gospels agree that Simon of Cyrene was forced into carrying the cross for Jesus. Mark gives the extra detail that Simon had two sons called Alexander and Rufus. The fact that he does not explain anything about them probably means that they were known to his audience. Perhaps they belonged to the Christian community in Rome.

(*Luke*: Luke includes a story about some women who wept for Jesus as he walked on his way to the crucifixion. Jesus told them not to weep for him but for themselves because the day would arrive when they would have enough troubles of their own. This is understood to be a reference to the coming destruction of Jerusalem in 70 AD.)

(b) **The crucifixion** (Mark 15:23–32; Matt. 27:33–44; Luke 23:33–43).

DEATH BY CRUCIFIXION

The victim was either nailed or tied to the cross beam by his wrists, before it was hoisted up and fixed into the permanent upright stake of the cross. The feet were also tied or nailed to the upright stake. The body was supported by a small block of wood at the bottom of the spine. Crucifixion was death by suffocation: the prisoner alternated between pushing himself upright in order to breathe and sagging back to rest and relieve the pain.

The following major points need to be noted about the crucifixion of Jesus:

1. Mark and Matthew record that, when the execution party arrived at Golgotha, Jesus was offered 'wine mixed with myrrh'. This was a drug that would ease the acute pain that crucifixion brought to the victim. Jesus refused it. Luke states that Jesus was offered 'sour wine' after he had been crucified.
2. All three Evangelists record that the soldiers divided Jesus' clothing by casting lots to see what each would get. This may well be a reference to Psalm 22:18.
3. Mark says it was nine o'clock in the morning when the crucifixion took place.
4. The name of the criminal was normally fixed on the cross. All three Evangelists agree that in the case of Jesus it said 'the King of the Jews'. Two others were executed with Jesus.
5. In Mark and Matthew, Jesus was mocked by:

    (a) those passing by;
    (b) the chief priests and Scribes;
    (c) the two criminals crucified with him.

    Their mockery consisted of two taunts:

    (a) Jesus had claimed to destroy the Temple and rebuild it in

three days. If he could do this then surely he could come down from the cross and save himself.
(b) If he was the Christ, the King of Israel, then let him come down from the cross and convince people.

In Luke, Jesus was mocked by:

(a) the Jewish leaders;
(b) the Roman soldiers;
(c) one of the criminals crucified with him.

The mockery consisted of the one major taunt: that Jesus should save himself because he was (i) the Messiah, the Chosen One; and (ii) the King of the Jews.

(c) The death on the cross (Mark 15:33–9; Matt. 27:45–54; Luke 23:44–48). All three Evangelists agree that the account of the death of Jesus begins with the comment about 'darkness' being over the 'whole land' from the sixth hour (12 noon) until the ninth hour (3.00 pm). Various suggestions have been made about the meaning of this darkness. Luke adds the extra comment about the failing of the sun's light. This has led to the suggestion that there was an eclipse of the sun. Another suggestion is that it was a fulfilment of a prophecy such as 'I will make the sun go down at noon and darken the earth in broad daylight' (Amos 8:9).

At the moment of Jesus' death the curtain of the Temple was torn in two from top to bottom. This curtain covered the entrance to the Holy of Holies. The Jews believed that the Holy of Holies was the place where God was to be found. This tearing of the curtain symbolised that the God who was hidden is now revealed to all people. The old religion of the Jews is now replaced.

Mark and Matthew end their story with the words of the centurion:

Truly this man was the Son of God (*Mark 15:39; Matt. 27:54*).

Luke's story closes with the centurion pronouncing the innocence of Jesus:

Beyond all doubt . . . this man was innocent (*Luke 23:47*).

THE SAYINGS OF JESUS FROM THE CROSS

Four of the seven sayings of Jesus from the cross appear in the Synoptic Gospels: one in Mark and Matthew, and three in Luke.

> **1** Eli, eli, lema sabachthani? ... My God, my God, why hast thou forsaken me? (*Mark 15:34; Matt. 27:46*).

This is a quotation from Psalms 22:1. Some people find it hard to accept that Jesus would utter such a cry of despair. They point to the triumphant end of the Psalm and suggest that Jesus was reciting the Psalm but died before he could finish it.

Other people find it easier to accept the fact that Jesus felt totally deserted in the moment of pain and agony just before death. Certainly the latter view is in keeping with the great emphasis on suffering in Mark's Gospel.

A third view interprets the words as a belief in God even in the agony of death. It may be that Mark's Church preserved the words for this very reason. For a Church suffering persecution the idea of a Jesus who still prayed and showed faith in God at the moment of death would be a great comfort to them in their own distress.

> **2** Father, forgive them; they do not know what they are doing (*Luke 23:34*).

According to Luke, Jesus said this as he was crucified. The main problem surrounding this saying is: for whom is Jesus asking God's forgiveness? There are three possible answers:

(a) the Jewish leaders who had secured his execution;
(b) the Roman soldiers who carried out the crucifixion;
(c) the whole of humanity, who had refused to listen to him, or to recognise that he was sent from God to bring all people back to himself.

> **3** ... today you shall be with me in Paradise (*Luke 23:43*).

One of the two criminals executed with Jesus began to mock him. The other rebuked his fellow victim and, recognising the innocence of Jesus, requested Jesus to remember him. Jesus rewarded the man with the promise of Paradise. Paradise was a word used for the Garden of Eden. It stood for a 'state of blessedness' reserved for good people, prior to the resurrection at the last day.

> **4** Father, into your hands I commit my spirit (*Luke 23:46*).

These were Jesus' last words according to Luke. They are a quotation from Psalms 31:5. The life of Jesus was over and now he returned his spirit to God. This is a very important moment in Luke's Gospel. Jesus had lived by the spirit of God. The spirit had:

(a) brought him into the world (Luke 1:34–35);
(b) been given to him at baptism (Luke 3:22);
(c) anointed him for his ministry (Luke 4:18–19).

(d) **The women at the crucifixion** (Mark 15:40–41; Matt. 27:55–56; Luke 23:49). In Mark and Matthew's Gospel, Jesus died alone. The disciples were not present for they had failed and run away (Mark 14:50). It is at this point that the women are introduced into the story to take over the role of the disciples. In Mark, they were to fail as well (Mark 16:8). They watched the crucifixion from a distance. The women named in the three Gospels were as shown in the table below.

(*Luke*: Luke records that all his friends stood at a distance, including the women who had followed him from Galilee (Luke 8:3).)

Mark	Matthew	Luke
Mary of Magdala	Mary of Magdala	Mary of Magdala
Mary the mother of James the younger and Joseph	Mary the mother of James and Joseph	Mary the mother of James
Salome	The mother of the sons of Zebedee	Joanna

The Burial (Mark 15:42–47; Matt. 27:57–61; Luke 23:50–56)

The burial of Jesus had to be completed by 6.00 pm since this is when the Sabbath began and it was forbidden to bury on the Sabbath. Joseph of Arimathaea, a member of the Sanhedrin who was obviously sympathetic to Jesus (Matthew claims he had become a secret disciple), went to Pilate and asked for the body of Jesus. The body was taken and laid to rest in Joseph's own tomb.

The women took note of where the body was laid to rest, intending to come back, after the Sabbath was over, to complete the burial arrangements.

It is important to note two points regarding this story:

1 Jesus was really dead.
2 It was known where he had been buried.

This was important to the early Christians because they faced the charges that Jesus was not really dead when he was taken down from the cross and that, even if he was, the women could have gone to the wrong tomb on the Sunday morning.

What the Evangelists Believe about the Death of Jesus

All the Evangelists agree that the death of Jesus was necessary. All three understand the death of Jesus in the following ways:

1. It was inevitable. This means that they saw the death of Jesus as part of God's plan. The evidence for this view is seen throughout the Synoptic Gospels (Mark 8:31; 9:1, 31; 10:33; Matt. 16:21, 28; 17:22; 20:18; Luke 2:34; 9:22, 44; 18:31–33; 22:21; 24:6, 46).
2. It was the result of being obedient to God. Jesus died because he accepted the plan of God. He is the one who willingly sets out to face danger in Jerusalem (Mark 10:32; Matt. 20:17). Luke records the event in the strongest way: Jesus was the one who

> ... set his face resolutely towards Jerusalem (*Luke 9:51*).

From the time of Peter's declaration of faith, the material of each of the Synoptic Gospels is written in the style of a journey to Jerusalem in order that the destiny of Jesus could be accomplished.

3. It was due to the wickedness of humanity. People refused to accept Jesus as the Messiah and as a result they rejected his authority (Mark 2:7, 20; 3:22; 14:10–11, 21; Matt. 9:3, 15, 12:24; 26:14–16, 24; Luke 5:21, 35; 6:11; 7:34; 11:15; 13:33; 22:2, 50).

Luke adds two further reasons for the death of Jesus:

4. It was the way in which repentance and forgiveness of sins could be offered to all people (Luke 24:47).
5. It was the way Jesus could be glorified. As Luke says in his chapter on resurrection:

> Was the Messiah not bound to suffer thus before entering upon his glory? (*Luke 24:26*).

What the death of Jesus means for Christians today

The suffering of Jesus was inevitable

While Christians see the suffering of Jesus as part of the whole human experience, they also see Jesus' suffering as inevitable in a unique way. He suffered opposition, rejection, hatred and death because of who he was and what he had come to do. This was inevitable because Jesus remained totally obedient to what he saw as the will of God for him. This obedience resulted in death because of the wickedness and sin of humanity.

Reconciliation

Christians believe that God sent Jesus into the world to show all people a way back to himself. Luke, especially, portrays Jesus as the perfect man, who set the perfect pattern of human life. When people attempt to live like Jesus reconciliation with God can take place. Reconciliation means coming back to God and living in harmony with him.

Throughout history there have been different theories about how the death of Jesus reconciles people to God. Some of them are not acceptable to all twentieth-century Christians.

(a) **God must be satisfied**. *In the Middle Ages, and even for some Christians today, the idea of reconciliation was based on the belief that God was offended by the sins of people. A punishment needed to be given. A debt to God needed to be paid. The only one who could pay such a debt was a perfect person because a sinful person would be unacceptable to God. So God sent his son as the victim who would satisfy God's sense of justice.*

Many Christians today would find such a theory totally distasteful. They do not believe in a God who is an unforgiving, cruel tyrant.

(b) **The ransom theory**. *Mark talks about Jesus giving*

> *... his life as a ransom for many (Mark 10:45).*

The word 'ransom' seems to indicate that a price had to be paid to God in order that he would free people from their sins.

Again, it is not surprising that most Christians find this theory totally unacceptable. If God is perfect in love and mercy, he does not need a ransom to be paid in order to allow people to return to him. His nature is not fickle. His nature is love and love does not make such demands.

(c) **Jesus gives his life as a ransom**. *This is a different theory to the previous one. Many Christians understand the word 'ransom' to mean 'belonging to God'. They would claim God showed such a great love for people that he even allowed Jesus to die on the cross in order that his love might persuade them to return and belong once more to him.*

Jesus as a sacrifice

At the Last Supper, Jesus said:

> This is my blood, the blood of the covenant, shed for many ...
> (Mark 14:24).
>
> This cup, poured out for you, is the new covenant sealed by my blood (Luke 22:20).

These two variants of the same words, one by Mark and the other by Luke, are very important for Christians today. The 'blood of the covenant' is a reference to the time of Moses. In those days, an animal was offered in sacrifice to God, and its blood was sprinkled over the people as a sign of the one blood of life shared between God and his people.

Many Christians do not see Jesus as a sacrifice in the same way. They do not think of him as a sacrifice offered to God. They see Jesus as freely giving his blood; that is, giving himself to all people. It is the gift of himself. Through him people are linked with God in the life of the covenant agreement.

In addition, Luke talks about the 'new covenant'. This is a reference to the prophet Jeremiah (31:31), where the prophet says that the agreement made with God will be written on people's hearts. The covenant will be an affair of the heart, not just blind obedience to the Law.

Death and Resurrection

Many Christians only see meaning in the death of Jesus if it is linked to the resurrection. Without the resurrection they do not see how the death of Jesus achieves much at all. Luke was one of the first Christians to understand the death of Jesus in this way. That is why he writes such comments as:

> Was the Messiah not bound to suffer thus before entering upon his glory? (*Luke 24:26*);

> ... the Messiah is to suffer death and to rise from the dead on the third day, and ... in his name repentance bringing the forgiveness of sins is to be proclaimed to all nations (*Luke 24:46*).

Christians see the power of God's love as so strong that it overcomes sin and death. Through both the death and resurrection of Jesus, humanity is now reconciled to God even if some people are unaware of, or do not care to hear, the good news.

Study Skills

Knowledge

1. What instructions did Jesus give for the preparation for the Passover?
2. Give an account of what happened at the Passover meal.
3. What happened in the Garden of Gethsemane?
4. In Mark's Gospel what did the High Priest ask Jesus at his trial before the Sanhedrin?
5. What answer did Jesus give?
6. Why did Jesus deserve to die according to the Jewish Law?
7. Who was the Roman Governor at this time?
8. Who carried Jesus' cross?
9. What does 'Golgotha' mean?
10. What happened to Jesus' clothes?

11 Who watched the crucifixion?
12 Who asked for the body of Jesus and buried it in the tomb?

Understanding

13 Do you think the Last Supper was a Passover meal? Give reasons for your answer.
14 What do you understand Jesus to mean by the words he spoke on the cross in the Synoptic Gospels?

Evaluation

15 'Pilate did not want to condemn Jesus.' Explain how and why the synoptic writers tried to excuse Pilate from the blame for Jesus' death.
16 'If Jesus had not been crucified there would have been no Christianity.' Do you agree with this statement? Give reasons for your answer.
17 Assess the various beliefs held by Christians about the death of Jesus.

Examination Practice

Read the following passage carefully, noting the words in italics, and answer the questions below it.

'The hour of the crucifixion was nine in the morning, and the inscription giving the charge against him read, *"The King of the Jews"*. Two bandits were crucified with him, one on his right and the other on his left.

'The passers-by hurled abuse at him: "Aha!" they cried, wagging their heads, "You would pull the Temple down, would you, and build it in three days? Come down from the cross and save yourself!" So too the chief priests and lawyers jested with one another: *"He saved others,"* they said, *"but he cannot save himself.* Let the Messiah, the King of Israel, come down now from the cross. If we see that, we shall believe." Even those who were crucified with him taunted him' (Mark 15:25–31).

(a) Why do you think the inscription 'King of the Jews' was put on the cross (4)
(b) Jesus was ridiculed by passers-by, their religious leaders and those crucified with him. Why was this? (4)
(c) 'He saved others.' Illustrate this saying by describing *one* incident when Jesus 'saved' other people during his life. (4)
(d) Mark put great emphasis on the death of Jesus. Explain the reasons for doing this. Why is this death important to Christians? (8)

Practical Work

- Find out how the different Christian Churches celebrate the last week of Jesus' life. Try to discover the emphasis they place on the crucifixion. This could be done either by inviting representatives of the Churches into school or by interviewing them outside school.

CHAPTER

7 The Resurrection of Jesus in the Synoptic Gospels

The purpose of this chapter is to try to discover what Mark, Matthew and Luke mean by the resurrection. There are two important questions to be discussed:

– What did the resurrection mean to the synoptic writers?

    1 The empty tomb (Mark 16:1–8; Matt. 28:1–8; Luke 24:1–12)
    2 The problem of the ending of Mark
    3 Matthew's own story (Matt. 28:9–10, 16–20)
    4 Luke's own story (Luke 24:13–53)

– What the resurrection means for Christians today

What Did the Resurrection Mean to the Synoptic Writers?

The Empty Tomb (Mark 16:1–8; Matt. 28:1–8; Luke 24:1–12)

The only account shared by the three synoptic Evangelists is the story of the empty tomb. The similarities and differences in the accounts can be summarised as follows:

1. All three agree that the women went to the tomb early on the Sunday morning.
2. Mark names the women as Mary of Magdala, Mary the mother of James, and Salome. Matthew omits Salome and mentions just the two Marys, referring to the second as 'the other Mary'. Luke substitutes Joanna for Salome and mentions that there were other women with them.
3. Matthew alone records that the stone was removed by the Angel of the Lord who put the guards to sleep, thereby giving the impression that they were dead.
4. In Mark, the women were discussing who would roll away the stone at the entrance of the tomb.
5. In Mark and Luke only, the women entered the tomb. In Luke

they did not know what to think because the body of Jesus was missing.
6 The message of resurrection was given by a young man in white in Mark, by two men in white in Luke, and by the Angel of the Lord in Matthew.
7 The message of resurrection is the same in all three Gospels:

> He is not here; he has risen.

However, in Mark and Matthew a further message was given to the disciples. They were to go to Galilee where Jesus would meet them. In Luke, no such message is given.
8 In Luke, the women told the Eleven what had happened but they were not believed. In Matthew they ran from the tomb with great joy to tell the disciples. In Mark they ran away from the tomb and said nothing at all because they were afraid.

Meaning

The main teaching of the story of the empty tomb is found in the message: 'He is not here; he has risen.' It is a teaching that is expressed simply, yet for Christians is at the very centre of their faith. Jesus had died on the cross on Friday but now he had risen from the dead.

The Problem of the Ending of Mark

The ending of Mark's Gospel presents problems. Not only does the Gospel end on a note of fear but Mark does not record one single resurrection appearance. For a long time it has been thought that Mark's Gospel is incomplete. When it is compared with the Gospels of Matthew and Luke, Mark's appears unfinished as both the others have resurrection appearances.

It is obvious that the early Christians thought the Gospel was incomplete because there were at least three attempts to 'finish' the Gospel, all of which are much later than Mark. The one that appears in most New Testaments is known as the *canonical ending* (Mark 16:9–20). This ending was not written by Mark and was probably written in the second century. It is a summary of events to be found in the other three Gospels.

Is Mark's Gospel Finished?

Various suggestions have been made as to why the Gospel of Mark seems unfinished. All the suggestions assume that there must have been more material and that Mark could not have ended his Gospel without a resurrection appearance. Each suggestion, however, can be seriously questioned.

(a) **The end of the Gospel was deliberately removed.** It has been suggested that the end of the Gospel was suppressed because of what Mark had written. It is difficult, however, to think of any story that might have been so offensive as to call for such action. This suggestion causes more difficulties than it solves.

(b) **The Gospel was mutilated accidentally.** It has been suggested that the ending of the Gospel was torn by accident. If so, why did not Mark, or one of his friends, repair the manuscript?

(c) **Mark died before he could finish his Gospel.** The suggestion has been made that Mark died or was killed before he could complete his Gospel. Certainly this was a possibility in the Rome of Mark's day. Once again, however, it is difficult to believe that the Gospel would have been released unfinished. Surely some disciple of Mark would have finished the book before it was given to the Church?

All these suggestions seem empty. Each assumes that there was in fact a lost ending to the Gospel. However, a further important fact needs to be considered. There is no evidence whatsoever that there ever was an ending following on from verse 8. The only text available in the Church ends with the words 'for they were afraid'. In view of the fact that Mark's Gospel circulated widely throughout the early Christian communities, it is even more surprising that there is no knowledge of any text going beyond 16:8 if, of course, such a text ever existed.

CONCLUSION ON THE ENDING

- Mark's Gospel may be unfinished but this is not proven.
- The claim that the Gospel is unfinished is based on assumptions that there must have been an ending. This cannot be proved.
- It is possible that the Gospel finished on a note of despair with the words 'They said nothing to anybody, for they were afraid' (Mark 16:8).

A Second Problem (Mark 16:7)

There is a second problem in the story of the empty tomb recorded by Mark. Mary of Magdala and her companions are told to go and tell Peter and the other disciples:

> He is going on before you to Galilee; there you will see him, as he told you (*Mark 16:7*).

There seems to be a direct contradiction between verse 7 and verse 8. In verse 7 the message is that the disciples will see Jesus in Galilee. In the next verse the women fail to deliver the message, so disobeying the command. It seems hard to believe that Mark meant such a contradiction. The answer to the problem depends on the interpretation of verse 7.

At first sight the verse seems to be referring to a resurrection appearance but some scholars believe it refers to something else yet to come. This is the Second Coming of Jesus, known as the *parousia*.

If this interpretation is applied then the ending of the Gospel does make sense. The phrase 'there you will see him' refers to the future; a future yet to happen and which therefore cannot be recorded. This message of the return of Jesus would have been of the utmost importance to Mark's readers, who lived in a time of persecution, who believed passionately in the fact that Jesus was alive and who longed for the Second Coming of Jesus when suffering and persecution would be no more.

SUMMARY

- There is no evidence that the Gospel ended in any other way than 'They said nothing to anybody, for they were afraid' (Mark 16:8). Therefore, it may be that Mark purposely does not include a resurrection appearance.
- The words 'He is going on before you into Galilee; there you will see him, as he told you' (Mark 16:7) could refer to the Second Coming of Jesus and not to a missing resurrection appearance.
- Perhaps Mark does not record a resurrection appearance because it would confuse the message of the Second Coming of Jesus.
- The message of resurrection is given in the story of the empty tomb.
- Mark's readers already believed that Jesus had risen from the dead and was with them every day. Living in a time of persecution, they longed for Jesus to return and put an end to their suffering.

Matthew's Own Story

Matthew does not follow the Markan view of the resurrection and goes on to give accounts of Jesus appearing in a risen form.

The Appearance to the Women (Matt. 28:9–10)

When a comparison is made between the accounts of the empty tomb in Mark and Matthew, one of the most striking differences is in the behaviour of the women. There is nothing in Mark except the dark picture of despair which ends in the failure to deliver the message of resurrection. Not so in Matthew. Any fear the women felt in Matthew's account is overcome by great joy. They run to tell the disciples.

This joy is reinforced by the first of Matthew's own stories. Jesus appeared to the women and re-emphasised the message of the angel:

> Go and tell my brothers that they must leave for Galilee; they will see me there (*Matt. 28:10*).

Meaning

For Matthew, Galilee is the place where the disciples will see the risen Lord and share in the joy of the resurrection.

The Appearance in Galilee and the Commissioning of the Eleven (Matt. 28:16–20)

Matthew's Gospel concludes with Jesus appearing to the eleven disciples in Galilee. There they were commissioned by Jesus for the work that lay ahead. They were to

> ... make disciples of all the nations; baptise them in the name of the Father and of the Son and of the Holy Spirit, and teach them to observe all the commands I gave you (*Matt. 28:18–19*).

In all their work Jesus promised to be with them until the end of time.

Meaning

The commissioning of the disciples in Matthew's Gospel is incredible in its depth and insight. Matthew offers this conclusion as a summary of Jesus' work and purpose.

1 All authority in heaven and on earth has been given to me (*Matt. 28:18*).

Through the resurrection, Jesus was given the authority that, up to then, had been the sole possession of God. He had already exercised this authority in his teaching but now his authority received the approval of God through the resurrection.

What is more important is that the authority of the risen Jesus is about to be put into practice by the Church acting on his behalf. This is clearly seen in the words of Jesus that follow:

2   Go, therefore, and make disciples of all the nations (*Matt. 28:19*).

Jesus had 'made' disciples at the beginning of his ministry, and throughout Matthew's Gospel they are seen as the future community of the Church. Indeed, on one of them, Simon Peter, the Church was to be founded (Matt. 16:18).

Now the disciples were to carry on the practice of calling people to belong to the community of God in the Church. They were to do this in two ways.

3   ... baptise them in the name of the Father and of the Son and of the Holy Spirit (*Matt. 28:19*).

Baptism soon became the means of initiation into the Christian Church. In this instruction of Jesus there is found the earliest use of the name of the Trinity in connection with the rite of entry into the Christian community. This is a rite which, throughout history, has been a distinctive feature of Christianity.

4   ... and teach them to observe all the commands I gave you (*Matt. 28:20*).

As Jesus had taught the disciples throughout his ministry, now they must make sure that those who were converted and brought to baptism were taught in the same way. Converts would make their response to the risen Lord by keeping all the commands Jesus gave. The Church assumed the role of teacher, following in the footsteps of Jesus.

5   And know that I am with you always; yes, to the end of time (*Matt. 28:20*).

Matthew's Gospel closes with a promise which expresses a most important Christian belief. This promise is not an isolated thought tacked on the end of the story as a happy ending. The promise is that the risen Jesus can always be found in the midst of the Church. However much the Church strays away from God, the presence of Jesus will still be found there until the end of time.

> *SUMMARY*
> - Matthew does not share Mark's view of the response of the women at the tomb. He records that they were filled with joy and ran to tell the disciples what had happened.
> - While they were on their way, Jesus appeared to them and re-emphasised the message that the disciples would find him in Galilee.
> - Jesus appeared to them in Galilee and commissioned the disciples for the world-wide mission that lay ahead. This account teaches that:
>   - (a) Jesus has been granted all authority that comes from God.
>   - (b) The disciples, acting as the Church, are to make disciples of all nations.
>   - (c) They are to use baptism as the initiation rite into the Christian community.
>   - (d) They are to teach converts the commandments of Jesus.
>   - (e) Jesus himself will be found in the life of the Church until the end of time.

Luke's Own Story

Luke, like Matthew, does not share Mark's view of the resurrection. He also goes on to give accounts of Jesus appearing in a risen form.

The Road to Emmaus (Luke 24:13–35)

This story only occurs in Luke. Two disciples, Cleopas and a friend, were on their way to a village called Emmaus when Jesus met them and walked with them. They did not recognise him. The two were obviously upset and explained to the stranger that Jesus, the man from Nazareth, had been crucified. They had hoped he would be the one to 'liberate Israel'. They were confused because some women had said that the tomb was empty and that they had received a message that Jesus was alive.

Jesus became quite angry with the two disciples and began to teach them how the scriptures said that the Messiah had to suffer before he could be glorified.

When they reached Emmaus, the two men invited Jesus to stay with them for supper. During the meal, as Jesus blessed and broke the bread, they recognised him but he disappeared from sight. They returned immediately to Jerusalem and told the Apostles, who in turn told them that they already believed that the resurrection had taken place because Jesus had appeared to Simon Peter.

Meaning

How much of this story is historical and how much it has been developed is difficult to decide. For many people there is one main difficulty with the story: why did the two disciples not recognise Jesus, especially in view of the fact that a long conversation took place between them? The story says 'something kept them from seeing who it was'. This seems to be outside normal human experience.

Some scholars have suggested that the story of the road to Emmaus, whatever its historical origins, has been developed for the purpose of teaching certain ideas about the resurrection. There are three important ideas:

(a) **Jesus was to suffer in order to enter his glory**. Luke considers the suffering of Jesus as a necessary prelude to the glory of the resurrection. He refers to this throughout the Gospel (see Luke 9:22; 18:31–33; 24:7, 46).

(b) **Jesus was the fulfilment of scripture**. Luke sees Jesus as the fulfilment of the scriptures. The Gospel follows this theme at all major points. For example, the infancy narratives (Luke ch. 1–2), the beginning of the ministry of Jesus in the synagogue at Nazareth (Luke 4:18–19) and the whole theme of suffering (Luke 9:22; 18:31–33; 24:7) are all seen as being the fulfilment of the Old Testament.

(c) **Jesus is recognised in the breaking of bread**. When Jesus is recognised in the blessing and breaking of the bread, the non-recognition earlier in the story makes sense. Luke is saying that people meet the risen Christ in the breaking of bread. Most scholars believe that Luke is making a link between the risen Christ and the Eucharist. Such a link cannot be historical as the Last Supper had only taken place some forty hours earlier and therefore the Eucharist had not yet become established as part of Christian worship.

Nevertheless many Christians believe that Jesus is present in the breaking of the Eucharistic bread. There he can be recognised and this happens because he has risen from the dead.

The Apologetic Legend (Luke 24:36–43)

While Cleopas and his companion were discussing the startling news of resurrection with the rest of the disciples, Jesus appeared to them. In spite of their discussions their immediate reaction was that they were seeing a ghost.

Jesus showed them his hands and feet and invited them to touch him. He then asked for something to eat and was given a piece of grilled fish which he ate in front of them.

Meaning

This story is known as the *Apologetic Legend*. This means that Luke wrote the passage with one purpose in mind: to convince his readers that Jesus rose from the dead in a physical sense. This was important to Luke. His readers were largely the Gentiles of the Roman Empire, who were greatly influenced by Greek culture. He did not want them to think of the resurrection of Jesus in the sense that any good man might be given a place with the gods in spirit form, which was what many Greeks believed. The resurrection of Jesus meant that he had returned in a physical form.

Last Instructions to the Apostles (Luke 24:44–49)

After eating the piece of fish, Jesus returned to instructing the Apostles. His teaching centred around two of the points already highlighted in the story of the two disciples on the road to Emmaus:

1 Jesus is the fulfilment of scripture.
2 The Messiah must suffer and rise again.

This was so that repentance for the forgiveness of sins might be preached to all nations, beginning from Jerusalem. He told them to stay in the city until they were given

> ...the power from above (*Luke 24:49*).

Meaning

The importance of this story to Luke's whole purpose cannot be overestimated. The meaning is quite clear:

1 The work of Jesus was completed. The disciples had now to begin their mission to the world. That mission was to offer repentance that would bring the forgiveness of God.
2 They had to start in Jerusalem. This is very important to Luke. The whole Gospel points towards Jerusalem as the place where the Christ must go, suffer and die, in order to rise from the dead and be glorified. Now, beginning from Jerusalem and moving out, the message of the Christ was to be preached to all. The missionary work of the Church was about to begin.
3 The beginning of this mission was to be marked by the disciples receiving the gift of the Holy Spirit. Then the spread of

Christianity could begin (Luke wrote a second book to show this missionary activity: the Acts of the Apostles).

The Ascension (Luke 24:50–53)

Jesus and his disciples went out to Bethany, a village some seven miles from Jerusalem. After blessing them, he was carried up to heaven. The disciples returned to Jerusalem, joyfully praising God.

Meaning

The ascension is a story to explain how Jesus returned to be with God when his work was over. The people of the time believed that God lived in heaven and that heaven was above the clouds. It was natural, therefore, for Jesus to ascend in order to return to God. Some Christians take the account literally. Others see it as a belief expressed in legendary terms.

SUMMARY

- The story of the Emmaus road teaches that:
    (a) Jesus, as the Messiah, had to suffer to rise from the dead and enter his glory.
    (b) Jesus is the fulfilment of all scripture.
    (c) Jesus is recognised in the breaking of the bread at the Eucharist.
- The resurrection does not mean that Jesus is a ghost. He rose in a physical form.
- The disciples were to commence a mission of preaching repentance for the forgiveness of sins to all nations.
- They were to begin in Jerusalem and to wait there until they had received the gift of the Holy Spirit.
- Jesus returned to be with God at the ascension.

What the resurrection means for Christians today

Christians accept that there is no historical proof of the resurrection. They accept that nobody witnessed the event. Yet the Christian faith stands or falls with the resurrection. It is important, therefore, to discover what Christians believe about this event.

The empty tomb

The only story that occurs in all three Synoptic Gospels is the story of the empty tomb. It is accepted by most Christians that this story proves nothing in itself.

The story has been surrounded by arguments since the very beginning of Christianity. Many different theories have been put forward to explain why the tomb was empty. Some of the theories are as old as Christianity itself; others are more modern. The main difficulty with the theories is that, even for non-Christians, they make little sense and are not widely accepted.

1 *Jesus was not really dead and revived in the cool of the tomb.*

Answer: It is difficult to imagine anyone being able to survive death by crucifixion, especially after first receiving scourging by the Roman authorities.

2 *The women went to the wrong tomb on the Sunday morning.*

Answer: All three Synoptic Gospels state that the women had seen where Jesus had been buried (Matt. 27:61; Mark 15:47; Luke 23:55). Even if they had gone to the wrong tomb, it is highly unlikely that someone would not have checked out their story. Indeed, Luke records that Simon Peter did just that (Luke 24:12). This theory would only begin to make sense if it is accepted that Peter also went to the wrong tomb.

3 *Someone stole the body of Jesus. There are only three groups of people who could have done this: the disciples, the Jewish leaders or the Roman authorities.*

Answer: There seems no sensible reason why the disciples should have stolen the body of Jesus. This was one of the earliest charges against the Christian Church and is the very question Matthew tried to answer in his story about the guard at the tomb. If the disciples did steal the body of Jesus then Christianity is based on a lie. It is extremely doubtful whether the disciples would be prepared to die for a lie. If either the Romans or the Jewish authorities stole the body, why did they not produce the evidence when the disciples began to preach about Jesus rising from the dead?

Theories such as these present no problem for Christians today because their faith is not based on the empty tomb. It is based on the resurrection. The empty tomb is secondary. It is the resurrection that makes sense of the empty tomb and not the empty tomb that proves the resurrection.

Did the resurrection happen?

Christians believe that Jesus rose from the dead. They believe this not just because there are stories in Matthew's and Luke's Gospels about Jesus appearing to his disciples after the resurrection. There is another reason. The existence of the Christian Church is based on the resurrection. All the Gospels agree that the disciples, prior to the resurrection, were worried and frightened men. Something happened to change that group of frightened men into men of courage; men who spoke out boldly in public and, if necessary, were prepared to die for their new-found faith. The disciples themselves said that the reason for their change of attitude was that they were convinced that Jesus was alive and with them. The existence of the Christian Church is due to the conviction that Jesus had risen from the dead. Both Matthew and Luke make this very clear (Matt. 28:16–20; Luke 24:47–49; Acts 2:32; 3:26; 4:10; 5:31; 10:40; 13:30; 17:31).

What happened?

It is impossible to say what happened at the moment of resurrection. Christians, therefore, differ in their views of what took place.

Some Christians have suggested that the resurrection did not happen at all. They claim that the disciples became aware of who Jesus was and what he had come to do only after his death and that they were inspired to carry on his work. The majority of Christians, however, cannot accept that the disciples suddenly believed in resurrection and began to preach a new faith based on what was, after all, an untruth.

Other Christians believe that Jesus rose in bodily form. He was not a ghost; he could be touched and could eat (Luke 24:41–43). The main weakness with such a narrow view is that it ignores some of the evidence found in the other Gospels. It seems to reduce the resurrection to the idea of a corpse coming back to life.

A third view, while accepting the bodily resurrection of Jesus, allows for other matters to be taken into consideration. There was something different about the risen Jesus. The disciples doubted (Luke 24:42). Jesus seemed able to come and go as he pleased in a way that was not normal (Luke 24:31). Above all he was recognised, worshipped and accepted in faith (Matt. 28:17; Luke 24:52). It would seem that for the first Christians, as for Christians of every age, faith was the only way to a full understanding of the risen Christ.

What does the resurrection mean?

- Christians believe that the resurrection proves the identity of Jesus. In short, a Christian is one who confesses that Jesus is Lord (see chapter 8).
- Christians believe that the resurrection completes the work of Jesus. His life and death were an attempt to bring all people back to God but people rejected him. Therefore Jesus had to suffer to achieve his purpose. This is what Luke means when he talks about Jesus having to suffer to enter his glory (Luke 24:26). God confirmed Jesus' work by raising him from the dead. Through the resurrection, forgiveness of sins can take place (Luke 24:47) and people can be restored to God.

- *Christians believe that Jesus rose into the life of the Church and that the Church has a duty to carry on the mission of Jesus. The Gospel must be preached to all nations. People must be baptised into the faith. They must be taught the way of Jesus (Matt. 28:16–20).*
- *Christians believe that the resurrection is not just an event of the past but has meaning for the present. They believe that Jesus is alive and with them day by day (Matt. 28:20). Many also believe that Jesus is especially present in the breaking of the Eucharistic bread (Luke 24:31).*
- *Christians believe that the resurrection means that death has been overcome. It is not the end. Jesus has triumphed over death and offers eternal life to those who follow him.*

Study Skills

Knowledge

1. According to the synoptic writers, who went to the tomb early on the Sunday morning?
2. Why did they go to the tomb?
3. In Mark's Gospel, the message of resurrection was given by a young man in white. According to Luke who gave the message to the women?
4. What was the message?
5. How does the message end?
6. Where were Cleopas and his companion going when they met Jesus?
7. According to Luke, why did they not recognise Jesus?
8. When did they recognise Jesus?
9. Who, according to Luke, saw the risen Jesus first?
10. How did Jesus prove he was not a ghost when he appeared to the eleven disciples?
11. What did Jesus say the disciples had to do?
12. What special gift did Jesus promise to send the disciples?
13. Where would they receive this gift?
14. According to Matthew's Gospel, where did Jesus meet his disciples?
15. What did Jesus commission them to do?
16. What promise did Jesus make to his disciples?

Understanding

17. What do you understand to be the problem with the ending of Mark's Gospel?
18. What do you think Luke is trying to teach about the risen Jesus in the story of the two disciples on the road to Emmaus?
19. Explain the words:
    '. . . in his name repentance bringing the forgiveness of sins is to be proclaimed to all nations. Begin in Jerusalem; it is you who are

witnesses to it all ... so stay in the city until you are armed with the power from above' (Luke 24:47–49).
20 What do you understand to be the task facing the Church, as a result of the commissioning of the disciples by the risen Jesus in Matthew's Gospel?

Evaluation

21 How important do you think belief in the empty tomb is to an understanding of resurrection?
22 Explain one difficulty a person might have in believing the resurrection. How would you answer that difficulty?

Examination Practice

Give a careful account of Luke's story of the empty tomb.	(6)
Why do you think the disciples did not believe the message the women told them when they returned from the tomb?	(4)
Outline briefly one other story about resurrection in Luke's Gospel.	(4)
What do Christians believe about the resurrection?	(6)

Practical Work

- In small groups, work out three simple questions on the resurrection. Each member of the group should then interview one or two adult Christians on the basis of the three questions. Then, in the groups, compile the results of this survey into belief about the resurrection.

CHAPTER

8 Who is Jesus?

The purpose of this chapter is to discover who the Evangelists think Jesus is. This also gives an insight into the belief of the first-century Christians about the person of Jesus. This can be done by examining the following:

- The major titles used of Jesus in the Synoptic Gospels
- The title used by Jesus himself in the Synoptic Gospels
- Other major titles used of Jesus

The Major Titles Used of Jesus in the Synoptic Gospels

The Christ

The title 'Christ' means 'anointed one'. *Christ* is a Greek word. In Hebrew the same word is *Messiah*. It is most important to realise that the words 'Messiah' and 'Christ' are the same word.

Jesus the Messiah (Hebrew)
Jesus the Christ (Greek)
Jesus the Anointed One (English)

All three mean the same. It is also important to realise that the word 'Christ' is a title given to Jesus. It is not a surname. To be accurate we should never say 'Jesus Christ' but rather 'Jesus *the* Christ'. Both Matthew and Mark use this title in the opening verses of their Gospels.

> A table of the descent of Jesus Christ . . . (*Matt. 1:1*).
>
> Here begins the Gospel of Jesus Christ . . . (*Mark 1:1*).

The background to the title is Jewish. In Israel, high priests and kings were anointed with oil as a sign that they had been chosen and appointed by God. The Jews believed their God was the only God. He was all-powerful; he controlled the destiny of all nations and peoples. This belief was severely tested after Israel was taken captive by the Babylonians in the sixth century BC.

During the period of exile, the Jews began to hope for the day when a leader would arise who would restore the nation to its former glory. They took to heart once more the promise of Moses, made a long time ago: 'The Lord your God will raise up a prophet from among you like myself, and you will listen to him' (Deuteronomy 18:15).

The idea of a Messiah figure gradually took shape. The main beliefs about him were:

1. He would be a descendant of David, chosen by God to rule as king.
2. He would be the representative of God who would protect the chosen people from all their enemies.
3. The holy city of Jerusalem and the holy Temple would become the centre of the world.
4. All the chosen people of Israel, wherever they were in the world, would be gathered into Palestine.
5. The Messiah would establish the rule of God on earth. This would bring about an age of perfect happiness and peace.

This was a magnificent hope but it did not last. By the time of Jesus, this belief in Messiahship had been watered down into a nationalistic hope for an earthly leader who would fight and drive out the Romans.

Mark, Matthew and Luke differ in their use of this title.

Mark

The title 'Christ' or 'Messiah' is rarely used in Mark's Gospel. At first it may seem surprising that the title 'Christ' does not appear more often in the Gospel. However, the explanation may be simple. Jesus did not speak of himself as Christ because he did not wish to be thought of as the popular military leader who would free Israel from the Romans.

(a) The only person in the Gospel to recognise Jesus, apart from the evil spirits, was Peter who, at Caesarea Philippi, made his profession of faith:

> You are the Messiah (*Mark 8:27–30*).

Jesus warns his disciples not to tell anyone. The explanation for this command of silence may well have been that Jesus did not want to be thought of as the popular Messianic figure who would drive out the Romans.

(b) Only at the end, during the trial before the Sanhedrin, did Jesus admit his Messiahship. The high priest asked,

> 'Are you the Messiah, the Son of the Blessed One?' Jesus said, 'I am; . . .' (*Mark 14:61*).

At this point in the Gospel there is nothing to be served by not using the title. Jesus knows that the end is near and that there can be no turning back.

Even though the actual title is rare Jesus did act as Messiah. For example, he rode into Jerusalem on Palm Sunday as a Messianic king:

> Hosanna! Blessings on him who comes in the name of the Lord! (*Mark 11:9; cf. Psalms 118:25–26*).

Matthew

Matthew is the Evangelist who writes specifically for the Jews. He is at pains to show Jesus as the Messiah. Some scholars regard his whole Gospel as being about the Messiahship of Jesus. They suggest that the Gospel divides into three separate sections:

(a) **The person of Jesus the Messiah** (Matt. 1:1–4:16). In this section Matthew shows how the new-born infant is the Messiah (see chapter 2).

(b) **The proclamation of Jesus the Messiah** (Matt. 4:17–16:20). Jesus shows himself to be Messiah by his teaching (Matt. ch. 5–7) and by his deeds (Matt. ch. 8–9) even though he is rejected. The section ends with Peter acknowledging Jesus as the Messiah (Matt. 16:16) and receiving the authority of Jesus to become the rock on which the Church would be built (Matt. 16:18).

(c) **The suffering and death of Jesus the Messiah** (Matt. 16:21–28:20). The third section forecasts the future rejection, suffering and death of Jesus who is the Messiah, and portrays the events of the last week and the death of the Messiah.

Luke

When Luke uses this title, he returns, in part, to the high hope of Judaism. Rather than weaken the idea of Messiahship, Luke adds to it and presents Jesus as the Messiah who has come not just for the Jews, but for all people.

(a) This was the purpose of the coming of Jesus. So at the birth of the baby in Bethlehem, the angel's message to the shepherds in the fields was one of Messiahship:

> Today in the city of David a deliverer has been born to you – the Messiah, the Lord (*Luke 2:11*).

(b) This view is supported by Simeon, in the Temple, at the time of Jesus' presentation. Simeon was a devout man who

> watched and waited for the restoration of Israel (*Luke 2:25*)

and had been promised that:

> he would not see death until he had seen the Lord's Messiah (*Luke 2:26*).

(c) Unlike the other Gospels, Luke claims that the beginning of Jesus' ministry happened, on Sabbath day, in the synagogue of his own village, Nazareth. He was chosen to read the lesson from the book of the prophets. The lesson for that day was from the prophet Isaiah (61:1–2) and the words are most significant:

> The Spirit of the Lord is upon me because he has anointed me;
> He has sent me to announce good news to the poor,
> to proclaim release for prisoners and recovery of sight to the blind;
> to let the broken victims go free,
> to proclaim the year of the Lord's favour (*Luke 4:18–19*).

Immediately after the lesson, Jesus rose to deliver the homily. His opening words were startling:

> Today, in your very hearing this text has come true (*Luke 4:21*).

What Jesus is claiming is that he is the Lord's anointed one: in other words, the Messiah. At first the words of Jesus were well received, but gradually the enthusiasm of the congregation gave way to cynicism as they realised that the speaker was, after all, the son of the local carpenter, Joseph.

Jesus, aware of their change of mood, gave two illustrations of his future Messiahship. First of all, he told them the story of Elijah and the widow of Sarepta. In the time of Elijah there had been a great famine, and Elijah had found refuge not amongst the Jews in Israel, but in Sarepta in the Gentile territory of Sidon. The second illustration was similar. In the prophet Elisha's time there were many lepers in Israel, but the only one Elisha cured was a Gentile called Naaman, from Syria. The congregation were furious with Jesus and hustled him out of the synagogue.

What Jesus was saying by the use of these two illustrations is that his Messiahship was for all people, not just the Jews. The kingdom of God would be set up not just amongst the faithful of the chosen people, but amongst all the faithful of every nation. This account highlights the theme of universalism found in Luke's Gospel.

(d) Later in the ministry of Jesus, John the Baptist sent two disciples to ask Jesus a direct question:

> Are you the one who is to come, or are we to expect some other? (*Luke 7:19; Matt. 11:3*).

Jesus' answer, based on the quotation from Isaiah which he read in the synagogue at Nazareth at the beginning of his ministry, makes it clear that Jesus is the Messiah:

> Go and tell John what you have seen and heard: how the blind recover their sight, the lame walk, the lepers are made clean, the deaf hear, the dead are raised to life, the poor are hearing the good news – and happy is the man who does not find me a stumbling-block (*Luke 7:22–23; Matt. 11:4–5*).

This is the role of the Messiah.

(e) Two of the references mentioning Jesus as Messiah are heavy with sarcasm. They are the taunts Jesus received, having been crucified:

> He saved others: now let him save himself, if this is God's Messiah, his Chosen (*Luke 23:35*).

> Are not you the Messiah? Save yourself and us (*Luke 23:39*).

(f) Twice, after the resurrection, Jesus admitted that he was the Messiah. On both occasions he was instructing his disciples: firstly, the two on the Emmaus road, and secondly, the eleven Apostles.

> Was not the Messiah bound to suffer thus before entering his glory? (*Luke 24:26*).

> This is what is written: that the Messiah is to suffer death and to rise from the dead on the third day, and that in his name repentance bringing the forgiveness of sins is to be proclaimed to all nations (*Luke 24:46–47*).

(g) In addition, there is a rare title used which also indicates the Messiahship of Jesus. The blind man at Jericho calls out:

> Jesus, Son of David, have pity on me! (*Mark 10:48; Matt. 20:30; Luke 18:38*).

It is meant to be understood that Jesus is the Messiah as the Jews believed that the Messiah would be a descendant of King David (Luke 1:32).

There is no doubt that, through the words and work of Jesus, the early Church came quickly to the belief that Jesus was the Messiah, the Christ of God, the anointed one.

Jesus: the Christ for today

Just as the Jews believed in a Messiah who would come to bring peace and establish the rule of God on earth, so Christians today see in Jesus that same

Messianic figure who has come and who has established and will establish God's kingdom on earth. The daily prayer of Christianity includes the words 'Your kingdom come, Your will be done, on earth as it is in heaven.'

The Jews also believed that the Messiah would free them from all their sufferings. Christians see Jesus the Messiah as the one who will lead them, and the whole world, through suffering and bring them and it back to God.

In our own day the world is not, at times, a happy place. Evils and injustices such as violence, poverty and starvation still bring suffering to many. The Christian disciple is committed to fighting all injustice. Outstanding examples of such discipleship can be found throughout history. Two such examples are Dr Albert Schweitzer, who struggled against leprosy in the damp disease-ridden forests of Africa, and the Rev. Dr Martin Luther King, who strived for equal human rights for all in the United States of America.

Today we find Mother Teresa of Calcutta working in the slums of India amongst extreme poverty. Other numerous Christian organisations continue to work in many areas of the world in the fight against starvation to bring in God's reign of justice and love.

It must be remembered that many non-Christian individuals and organisations also work against these injustices because of their own beliefs about the world and our place in it.

The Christian is commanded as a follower of the Christ to stand against the evils in the world, to speak out against all injustice and to work for the peace and harmony of all people under God.

The Son of God

The title 'Son of God' is the most popular title given to Jesus and it has been so for 2000 years.

The origin of the title is to be found in the Old Testament, where the nation of Israel is often referred to as God's son. In the prophet Hosea, for example, God says,

'When Israel was a boy, I loved him;
I called my son out of Egypt' (Hosea 11:1).

By the time of Jesus the 'Son of God' was seen as a Messianic title. Early in the history of Christianity, it became a title that went beyond that of the Messiah. It expressed the closest possible relationship between God and Jesus. This relationship is seen clearly in the Gospel accounts.

The Birth of Jesus
Even before the birth of Jesus the announcement of his sonship was

made by the angel to Mary. Her child would be special to God; born in a special way:

> The Holy Spirit will come upon you, and the power of the Most High will overshadow you; and for that reason the holy child to be born will be called 'Son of God' (*Luke 1:34–35*).

The Baptism of Jesus

The next occasion when the title is used is at the baptism of Jesus. Luke's account is somewhat strange in that it does not actually state that Jesus was baptised by John the Baptist. In fact in the previous paragraph it says that John had been imprisoned by Herod Antipas for criticising his relationship with Herodias, who was married to his half brother. Luke emphasises the part played by the Holy Spirit rather than the baptism itself.

At the moment of baptism, however, all three Evangelists describe how the voice of God spoke to Jesus about the close relationship between them:

> Thou art my Son, my Beloved; on thee my favour rests (*Mark 1:11; Matt. 3:17; Luke 3:22*).

These words come from two different parts of the Old Testament. 'Thou art my Son, the Beloved' is a quotation based on Psalm 2, a Messianic Psalm that talks about the Messiah coming to reign over Israel. 'On thee my favour rests' is a quotation from the Suffering Servant Songs of Isaiah (Isaiah 42), and by inference shows that the Messiah will be one who will suffer.

So Jesus is confirmed at one and the same time as both a Messianic figure and a figure who will experience suffering. He will do this because he is God's son.

Recognised by Evil

(a) It is interesting that the forces of evil seem to have no difficulty in recognising the person of Jesus. Early in the Gospel Luke records this general summary:

> At sunset all who had friends suffering from one disease or another brought them to him; and he laid his hands on them one by one and cured them. Devils also came out of many of them, shouting, 'You are the Son of God.' But he rebuked them and forbade them to speak, because they knew that he was the Messiah (*Luke 4:40–41*).

(b) Immediately after his baptism, Jesus went out into the wilderness and was tempted by the Devil. The story of the three temptations is a way of introducing the ministry of Jesus, for they are all to do with the question of how Jesus was to accomplish his mission. Many people believe that the best way of interpreting the temptations is to see them as the turmoil going on in the mind of Jesus rather than as a conversation with the Devil in person. The Devil stands for the force of evil in the world which all people experience.

1   If you are the Son of God, tell this stone to become bread (Matt. 4:3; Luke 4:3).

The Devil recognised Jesus and tempted him to use his power not only to satisfy his own hunger, but also as a means of persuading people to follow him. Jesus resists the temptation by quoting the Old Testament book of Deuteronomy (8:3):

Man cannot live on bread alone (*Matt. 4:4; Luke 4:4*).

2   In the second temptation (the third in Luke), Jesus was taken to the parapet of the Temple in Jerusalem.

If you are the Son of God, throw yourself down; for Scripture says, 'He will give his angels orders to take care of you' (*Matt. 4:6; Luke 4:10*).

Jesus was tempted to use his powers to perform incredible and magical tricks in order to make people respond to him and accept him. The reply of Jesus was, once again, from the book of Deuteronomy (6:16).:

You are not to put the Lord your God to the test (*Matt. 4:7; Luke 4:12*).

3   In the third temptation (the second in Luke), the Devil showed Jesus 'in a flash' all the kingdoms of the world and promised him total power if he would only do homage and worship him. The Son of God was being tempted to turn his back on God and become an advocate for evil. This was a real temptation, for Jesus could have used such powers to become a powerful world leader. Jesus rejected the temptation because it would have meant turning his back on God:

You shall do homage to the Lord your God and worship him alone (*Matt. 4:10; Luke 4:8*).

The Son of God was not to give in to such temptations and so the Devil left him.
  (c) It is also interesting that, in two separate stories about

exorcism, the evil spirits recognise Jesus as Son of God. They use, in each case, rare titles which are variants on the 'Son of God'.

1   In the story of the Capernaum demoniac, the possessed man shouts,

> What do you want with us, Jesus of Nazareth? Have you come to destroy us? I know who you are – the Holy One of God (*Mark 1:24; Luke 4:34*).

This is very near to calling Jesus the Son of God.

2   In the story of the Gerasene demoniac, Legion shouts,

> What do you want with me, Jesus, son of the Most High God? (*Mark 5:7; Matt. 8:29; Luke 8:28*).

The Transfiguration (Mark 9:2–8; Matt. 17:1–8; Luke 9:28–36)

When Jesus, accompanied by Peter, James and John, went up a mountain to pray, he was seen in a visionary state with Moses and Elijah. These two men were the holy representatives of Judaism. Moses was the great leader and Law-giver; Elijah was the great prophet. Elijah was supposed to return to prepare the way for the Messiah. In one sense also the Jews looked for a new Moses. Jesus is seen to be talking to both of them. Luke is the only Evangelist to say what they were talking about. He claims they were discussing his

> ... departure, the destiny he was to fulfil in Jerusalem (*Luke 9:31*).

This means Jesus' death. A cloud covered the scene and the voice of God, with words similar to those used at the baptism, said,

> This is my Son, My Beloved; listen to him (*Mark 9:7; Matt. 17:5; Luke 9:35*).

After this Jesus was found to be alone. Moses and Elijah had disappeared and the focus of attention had switched completely to Jesus. He is the Son of God – so listen to him.

The Father and the Son

In one short sentence, Matthew and Luke record the close relationship between Jesus and God:

> Everything is entrusted to me by my Father; and no one knows who the Son is but the Father, or who the Father is but the Son, and those to whom the Son may choose to reveal him (*Matt. 11:25–27; Luke 10:22*).

This mutual understanding between Father and Son is thought to be from a separate source and is more like the style found in John's Gospel.

The Parable of the Wicked Husbandmen

> What am I to do? I will send my own dear son; perhaps they will respect him (*Luke 20:13; Mark 12:6; Matt. 21:37*).

This parable deals with the theme of the salvation history. The son is sent by the owner of the vineyard (God) after all attempts to communicate with the tenants (Jewish leaders) through the servants (prophets) have failed. This was to fail too for the tenants

> flung him out of the vineyard and killed him (*Luke 20:15*).

Once again the parable indicates the close relationship enjoyed between Jesus and God.

Jesus before the Sanhedrin

The last occasion where the title is recorded is during the trial of Jesus before the Sanhedrin. In Mark and Matthew the high priest asked Jesus:

> Are you the Messiah, the Son of the Blessed One? (*Mark 14:61; Matt. 26:63*).

In Luke the chief priests and Doctors of the Law asked Jesus:

> You are the Son of God then? (*Luke 22:70*).

in response to which Jesus implied that he was. Jesus was condemned for speaking blasphemy.

SUMMARY

The meaning of the title 'Son of God' in the Gospels is that Jesus is a special person.

- a person in the tradition of the Old Testament;
- a person born through the creative power of the Holy Spirit;
- a person chosen by God and given a mission;
- a person recognised by evil;
- a person who had to resist evil;
- a person who enjoyed the closest possible relationship with God;
- a son, special beyond words.

Jesus: the Son of God for today

Many people have difficulty in understanding what God is really like. This is not surprising. God is not a human being. Even when God is called 'Father', it is only an image that is being used. Unlike a human father, God is everywhere; he is all-powerful; he is perfect. Such ideas have always been hard for people to understand.

Christians believe that Jesus provides the answer to the question: what is God really like? When they look at Jesus, he is like a window through which they can see God. Jesus is someone whom ordinary people can understand, yet he mirrors the perfect qualities of God.

For example, God's love for people is shown in the way that Jesus cared for those who were sick or outcasts from society, such as the tax-collector (Mark 2:15–17; Luke 19:1–10) or the woman who was a sinner (Luke 7:36–50).

God's desire for all people to come to him is shown in the way that Jesus was willing to die to convince them of his love. Christians believe Jesus did this because he was the 'Son of God'.

What the early Christians meant by calling Jesus the 'Son of God' was that they saw God at work in him; in his life, death and resurrection. So they could say, as did the centurion,

> Truly this man was a son of God (*Mark 15:39*).

The Title Used by Jesus Himself in the Synoptic Gospels

Son of Man

This is the title which is used only by Jesus. No one else, not even the authors in their editorial narrative, use it of Jesus. Many scholars believe it to be the most authentic title for this very reason.

Perhaps Jesus called himself by this uncommon name so that he could accomplish his mission to

> seek and save the lost (*Luke 19:10*)

without making an open claim to be the Messiah. Such a claim might have been misunderstood or might even have brought about a speedy end to his ministry.

The title 'Son of Man' has its origin in the Old Testament where there were two distinct ways to interpret the title.

1   In the earliest Hebrew poetry it simply meant 'a man' or 'man' in general:

... what is man that though shouldst remember him, mortal man (literally Son of Man) that thou shouldst care for him? (Psalms 8:4).

2   In the Old Testament book of Daniel, the phrase takes on a special meaning. In chapter 7 there is an account of one of Daniel's visions. He saw four great beasts appear from the sea. They were savage and terrifying. Then he saw an old man sitting as though in judgment and 'one like a son of man' (Daniel 7:13) was presented to him on 'the clouds of heaven'. He was brought before the old man, honoured by him and given power, glory and sovereignty.

The author of the book of Daniel gives an interpretation of the vision. The beasts stand for the nations such as Babylon which had conquered the Jews, and the figure of the Son of Man represented 'the saints of the Most High'. These were God's loyal few, who were ready to suffer and die rather than deny their faith in God. They would be given their place in heaven.

(a) In Matthew's and Luke's Gospels, but not in Mark, Jesus seems to use the title 'Son of Man' in the first of these Old Testament ways. There are three occasions where Jesus, in speaking of himself, seems to use the title just to mean himself as a man.

1   He uses it to speak of his mission:

> ... the Son of Man has come to seek and save what is lost (*Luke 19:10*).

2   He uses it when commenting on the cost of discipleship:

> Foxes have their holes, the birds their roosts; but the Son of Man has nowhere to lay his head (*Matt. 8:20; Luke 9:58*).

3   He uses it when criticising the people for their negative reaction to him:

> The Son of Man came eating and drinking, and you say 'Look at him! a glutton and a drinker, a friend of tax-gatherers and sinners!' (*Matt. 11:19; Luke 7:34*).

(b) All three Evangelists have many references that show that Jesus thought of himself as the Son of Man in the Daniel sense. They carry the idea of Jesus being cast in the role of the one who will come in power and glory on 'the clouds of heaven' at the end of time. This Second Coming of Jesus is called the *parousia*.

1   The first is from a passage on what it means to be a disciple:

> If anyone is ashamed of me and mine in this wicked and godless age, the Son of Man will be ashamed of him, when he comes in the glory of the Father and of the holy angels (*Mark 8:38; Matt. 16:27; Luke 9:26*).

2   The reverse is also true. Later in the Gospel, Jesus says to his friends:

> ... everyone who acknowledges me before men, the Son of Man will acknowledge before the angels of God (*Luke 12:8*).

3   Jesus tells his disciples to be ready for the coming of the Son of Man, for he will come unexpectedly:

> Hold yourselves ready, then, because the Son of Man will come at a time you least expect him (*Matt. 24:44; Luke 12:40*).

4   The Pharisees asked Jesus when the kingdom of God would come. They were told that it was not possible to observe the signs of its coming; in fact, it was already present (Luke 17:20–21). Jesus then went on to teach his disciples about the signs of the coming of the Son of Man. It will happen suddenly like a flash of lightning:

> The time will come when you long to see one of the days of the Son of Man, but you will not see it ... For like the lightning-flash that lights up the earth from end to end, will the Son of Man be when his day comes. But first he must endure much suffering and be repudiated by this generation (*Luke 17:22–25; Matt. 24:27*).

Then Jesus gave two illustrations about the suddenness of this future event. At the time of Noah, life went on without thought of danger right up until the time of the great flood. Life in the wicked city of Sodom went on right up to the day it was destroyed:

> ... it will be like that on the day when the Son of Man is revealed (*Matt. 24:37–41; Luke 17:26–30*).

5   The next verse comes from the apocalyptic passage found in all three Synoptic Gospels. In this Jesus is talking about the signs that will accompany the end of the world:

> Then they will see the Son of Man coming in the clouds with great power and glory ... (*Mark 13:26; Matt. 24:30; Luke 21:27*).

A few verses later the disciples are told, once again, to be alert because the timing of the end is a secret. No one knows when it will happen:

> Be on the alert, praying at all times for strength to pass safely through all these imminent troubles and to stand in the presence of the Son of Man (*Luke 21:36*).

6   The last of the references to the Son of Man which are related

directly to Daniel was at the trial before the Sanhedrin. Jesus was asked if he was the Messiah. Jesus did not answer this question but told the Jewish leaders:

> ... you will see the Son of Man seated at the right hand of God and coming with the clouds of Heaven (*Mark 14:62; Matt. 26:64; Luke 22:69*).

There are two more 'Son of Man' sayings in the Gospels concerning the question of authority. They claim that the authority of Jesus came from God, for Jesus claimed to do things that only God can do. In this way he is acting as the divine representative of God in the Daniel sense. The first is from the healing of the paralysed man:

> ... the Son of Man has the right on earth to forgive sins (*Mark 2:10; Matt. 9:6; Luke 5:24*).

The second is from a passage where Jesus and his disciples are criticised for breaking the Sabbath law. Jesus claimed his authority was greater than the Sabbath law:

> ... the Son of Man is sovereign even over the Sabbath (*Mark 2:28; Matt. 12:8; Luke 6:5*).

All the other sayings about the Son of Man in the Synoptic Gospels deal with the themes of suffering, death and resurrection. This is only a small part of the theme of the book of Daniel. There are eight such sayings found in the Markan source:

1. ... and he began to teach them that the Son of Man had to undergo great sufferings, and to be rejected by the elders, chief priests, and doctors of the law; to be put to death, and to rise again three days afterwards (*Mark 8:31; Luke 9:22*).

2. After the transfiguration Jesus warned the disciples

   > ... not to tell anyone what they had seen until the Son of Man had risen from the dead (*Mark 9:9; Matt. 17:9*).

3. ... the Son of Man ... is to endure great sufferings and to be treated with contempt (*Mark 9:12; Matt. 17:12*).

4. The Son of Man is now to be given up into the power of men, and they will kill him, and three days after being killed, he will rise again (*Mark 9:31; Matt. 17:22; Luke 9:44*).

5. We are going up to Jerusalem ... and the Son of Man will be given up to the chief priests and the doctors of the law; they

will condemn him to death and hand him over to the foreign power. He will be mocked and spat upon, flogged and killed; and three days afterwards, he will rise again (*Mark 10:33–34; Matt. 20:18; Luke 18:31*).

6 For even the Son of Man did not come to be served but to serve, and to give up his life as a ransom for many (*Mark 10:45; Matt. 20:28*).

7 At the Last Supper Jesus told his disciples:

The Son of Man is going the way appointed for him in the scriptures (*Mark 14:21; Matt. 26:24; Luke 22:22*).

8 In the Garden of Gethsemane Jesus says to his disciples:

The hour has come. The Son of Man is betrayed to sinful men. Up, let us go forward! My betrayer is upon us (*Mark 14:41–42; Matt. 26:45*).

In addition there are two sayings found in Luke's Gospel which follow the same theme:

1 The first warns the disciples that they, like Jesus, can expect nothing but hatred and suffering:

How blest you are when men hate you, when they outlaw you and insult you, and ban your very name as infamous, because of the Son of Man (*Luke 6:22*).

2 At the resurrection, the two men in white who deliver the message of resurrection to the women recall what Jesus had told them previously:

Remember what he told you while he was still in Galilee, about the Son of Man: how he must be given up into the power of sinful men and be crucified, and must rise again on the third day (*Luke 24:6–7*).

The main theme in these passages is suffering; far more than is to be found in the ideas of Daniel. We must look elsewhere for an answer to the question of what Jesus meant by the use of the title 'Son of Man'.

There is, however, another Old Testament book where the answer might be found. In Isaiah there is a collection of songs or poems about someone who is known as 'the Servant of the Lord'. These passages are sometimes called the 'Suffering Servant Songs' and the person in them is called 'the Suffering Servant'. It would seem that Jesus combined the idea of the Son of Man from Daniel with the Suffering Servant of Isaiah. In Isaiah 53, for example, the picture of the Servant fits neatly with the words and experience of Jesus: 'He was despised . . . tormented and humbled by suffering; we despised him . . . Yet on himself he bore our sufferings' (Isaiah 53:3–4). His suffering was not of his own making but was a punishment for the sins of others. This was the role of both the Suffering Servant and Jesus.

> For even the Son of Man did not come to be served but to serve, and to give up his life as a ransom for many (*Mark 10:45; Matt. 20:28*).

This joining of the functions of the Son of Man in Daniel and the Suffering Servant in Isaiah is unique to the Gospels. It has no parallel in Jewish literature. Many people think that the person responsible was Jesus himself.

SUMMARY

The title 'Son of Man' is used in three ways in the Synoptic Gospels:

- to refer to Jesus' own human situation;
- to refer to Jesus' return as judge, in power and glory, to set up the rule of God on earth (the theme of Daniel);
- to refer to Jesus' suffering, death and resurrection, to save people from their sins (the theme of Isaiah).

It must be remembered that this is the title Jesus uses of himself. Nowhere is Jesus called Son of Man by anyone else.

Jesus: the Son of Man for today

What relevance does Jesus, as Son of Man, have for people today? This is the most difficult title for twentieth-century Christians as they rarely use the title in everyday thinking and speaking about Jesus. However, the title is of great importance.

The title 'Son of Man' still tells of a time when Jesus will return and assist in judgment. There is a tendency today to think that everyone will finally be with God in heaven; that his love is so great that he will not turn anyone away. Others tend to think of God as someone who takes delight in condemnation. They look forward to the time when Jesus will return and exercise judgment on a wicked world.

The truth lies inbetween these two extreme views. The New Testament speaks of both God's mercy and his judgment. It warns of a time when humanity will be faced with judgment. The disciple who is 'ashamed' of Jesus will face the same treatment at the time of judgment (Mark 8:38; Matt. 16:27; Luke 9:26).

This idea of judgment makes sense when placed alongside the suffering of the Son of Man. Jesus suffered, died and rose again to save people from the power of sin. This has always been a fundamental belief of Christians. They believe that Jesus came to call all people back to God. His opening words in Mark's Gospel are a summary of his whole message:

> The time has come: the Kingdom of God is upon you; repent, and believe the Gospel (*Mark 1:15*).

This message of God's love was ignored and, instead of being accepted Jesus was rejected and executed. By his death, however, he showed the full extent of God's love. He was willing to die to show people how much God wished them to belong to him.

This sacrifice of Jesus, however, was to end not in death but in resurrection. As Mark says,

> The Son of Man is now to be given up into the power of men, and they will kill him, and three days after being killed, he will rise again (*Mark 9:31*).

So Christians believe that a person who responds to this message of the death and resurrection of Jesus can be united with God and saved from the power of evil which is called sin. This is what it means to call Jesus 'Son of Man'.

Other Major Titles Used of Jesus

Saviour

This is the rarest title in the Gospel. It does not occur at all in Matthew and Mark and is found only once in Luke:

> Today in the city of David a deliverer (Saviour) has been born to you – the Messiah, the Lord (*Luke 2:11*).

The title means that Jesus is seen as the one who can bring people back to God through his life, death and resurrection. Such people are 'saved' from evil and live with God both now and in eternity.

Jesus: Saviour for today

Most Christians believe that people are cut off from God. The main problem is human nature which falls far short of the perfection of God. Even when men and women try, by discipline, law or good works, to draw near to God, they are doomed to fail. They claim that, in Jesus, God has shown his love for all men and women.

This love was rejected and Jesus was killed. But God would not allow his love to be blotted out and raised Jesus from the dead. To anyone who receives the Christian faith, he offers salvation. Salvation is not something to be earned. It is not a reward. It is a free gift of God.

Some Christians claim that God's free gift must apply to all and that means everybody will be saved in the end. Others point out that, while the gift is given to all, a response is called for. This response is repentance and faith.

Lord

The early Church gave this title to Jesus after the resurrection. By the time the Gospels were written, the title was in common usage. It is not really surprising that Luke and Matthew, therefore, use the title. It is used in two ways in the Gospel:

1 It is used simply as a word meaning 'sir' or 'master'. When the leper came to Jesus he said,

> Sir, if only you will, you can cleanse me (*Luke 5:12*).

2 It is used as a word of adoration and praise. The message of the angel to the shepherds at the birth of Jesus was

> Today in the city of David, a deliverer has been born to you, the Messiah – the Lord (*Luke 2:11*).

Jesus: Lord for today

This title is still used today by the majority of Christians as a title of adoration. The title expresses the view that Christ's rule is over everything, a rule that will one day be recognised throughout the world. He is Lord of all creation. Modern Christians would agree with the earliest statement of belief in Christianity, stretching back to the earliest Church: Jesus is Lord.

SUMMARY

There are three main titles in the Gospels. One only appears on the lips of Jesus. The other two are used of Jesus in the Gospel narrative:

- Jesus is the Messiah – the Christ, anointed by the spirit of God. He was chosen to bring all people back to God. This

> Messiah would suffer and be put to death and rise again.
> - Jesus is the Son of God. He enjoys a unique relationship with God, his father.
> - Jesus is the Son of Man. He is one who must suffer and die but who will be raised from the dead. He will be given power and will return in glory to assist in God's judgment and the setting up of God's kingdom on earth.
>
> Further to the three main titles, Luke introduced two others that were to become important to the Church in the earliest years and ever since:
>
> - Jesus is Saviour. He offers freedom from sin and a return to God.
> - Jesus is Lord; Lord of all creation.

Study Skills

Knowledge

1. According to Luke, which title did Jesus use to refer to himself?
2. Which Old Testament book talks about the 'Son of Man'?
3. Which Old Testament prophet writes about the Suffering Servant?
4. Give an account of the theme of suffering contained in the sayings of the Son of Man in Luke's Gospel.
5. What do the words 'Christ' and 'Messiah' mean?
6. What did the Jews expect the Messiah to do?
7. In which two stories does God call Jesus his son?
8. On which occasion, in Luke's Gospel, is Jesus called deliverer or Saviour?
9. In the account of the temptations, what was Jesus tempted to do?
10. What did John the Baptist preach about the coming of Jesus?
11. What question did the disciples of John the Baptist ask Jesus when John sent them to him?
12. Give an account of the teaching of Jesus in the synagogue at Nazareth.

Understanding

13. At the time of Jesus some Jews held a popular idea of the role of the Messiah. What was this idea? How did Jesus show he was different from their expectation?
14. Explain the importance of the title 'Son of Man' for Jesus. How does Jesus combine this title with Isaiah's prophecies about the Suffering Servant?

Evaluation

15 What does it mean for Christians today to believe that Jesus was the Son of God?
16 In what ways do you think the title 'Son of Man' is important for Christians today?

Examination Practice

'He stood up to read the lesson and was handed the scroll of the prophet Isaiah. He opened the scroll and found the passage which says,
   "The spirit of the Lord is upon me because he has anointed me;
   he has sent me to announce good news to the poor,
   to proclaim release for prisoners and recovery of sight for the blind;
   to let the broken victims go free,
   to proclaim the year of the Lord's favour."
He rolled up the scroll, gave it back to the attendant, and sat down; and all eyes in the synagogue were fixed on him. He began to speak: "Today", he said, "in your very hearing this text has come true."'

What is the Hebrew word for 'anointed one'?	(1)
What did Jesus mean by saying that the text had come true even as they were listening?	(8)
Name another occasion when Jesus was called either 'God's anointed' or 'his chosen one'	(1)
What do you think is the importance of this story to Luke?	(4)
How important is it for Christians today to believe that Jesus is the anointed one of God?	(6)

Practical Work

- Arrange for one or two representatives or religious leaders such as a Roman Catholic priest, an Anglican priest or a Nonconformist minister to give a series of short talks and to answer questions on the subject of 'Who is Jesus?'
- Choose one of the following Christians: Dr Albert Schweitzer; the Rev. Dr Martin Luther King; Mother Teresa of Calcutta. Find out how he or she has tried to follow Jesus in his or her life and work.

Index of Gospel References

Mark

1:1–13	10	4:35–41	58, 70–72
1:1	136	4:38	18, 71
1:9–11	59	4:39	71
1:11	96, 142	4:40	71
1:12–13	59	4:41	71
1:14–9:50	10		
1:14–20	76–77	5:1–20	58, 59–61
1:15	152	5:3–4	60
1:17	76	5:7	144
1:21–28	58–59	5:15	60
1:21	59	5:19	60
1:22	59	5:21–24	58, 69–70
1:24	58, 144	5:25–34	58, 65–66, 67
1:25	58, 59	5:34	56, 66
1:27	59	5:35–43	58, 69–70
1:32–34	59	5:36	69
1:35–39	59	5:40	69
1:40–45	57, 58, 63–64, 67		
1:40	63	6:30–44	58, 72
1:41	56, 63	6:39	18
1:48	140	6:41	72
		6:45–8:13	11
2:1–12	57, 67, 76, 79–81	6:45–52	58, 72–73
2:3–12	10	6:50	73
2:7	117	6:51–52	73
2:10	85, 149		
2:13–14	76–77	7:24–30	58, 61–62
2:15–17	146	7:27	61
2:16–17	76, 81–82	7:28	61
2:17	8, 82, 85		
2:18–22	76, 82	8:27–9:1	76, 77–79
2:19	85	8:27–30	137
2:20	117	8:29	77
2:23–28	76, 83	8:31	117, 149
2:27	83	8:33	78
2:28	83, 85, 149	8:34	78
		8:35	79
3:1–6	76, 83–86	8:38	147, 152
3:4	85	8:47	66
3:6	18		
3:22	117	9:1	117
		9:2–8	144
		9:7	144

9:9	149
9:12	149
9:31	117, 149, 152
10:1–52	10
10:32	117
10:33–34	150
10:33	117
10:45	118, 150, 151
10:46–52	58, 66–67
10:47	66
10:52	67
11:1–16:8	10
11:1–11	91, 93–94
11:9	138
11:10	93
11:12–14	91, 94
11:15–19	91, 94–95
11:17	95
11:18	95
11:20–26	92, 95
11:27	95
11:27–33	92, 95–96
11:28	95
11:30	96
12:1–12	92, 96–97
12:6	145
12:13–17	92, 98
12:14	98
12:17	98
12:18–27	92, 98–99
12:26	99
12:27	99
12:28–34	92, 99–100
12:29–30	99
12:31	99
12:35–37	92, 100
12:38–40	92, 100
12:41–44	92, 100
13:26	148
14:1–2	92, 101
14:1	101
14:3–9	92, 102
14:10–11	92, 102, 106, 117
14:2	102
14:12–16	92, 104
14:17–21	92, 106–108
14:20	106
14:21	117, 150
14:22–25	92, 106, 107
14:22	106
14:24	106, 118
14:26–31	92, 107–108
14:26	106
14:32–42	92, 108–109
14:33	108
14:36	108
14:41–42	150
14:43–52	92, 109
14:50	109, 116
14:51	14
14:53–65	92, 110–111
14:53	110
14:55	110
14:56–57	110
14:59	110
14:61	137, 145
14:62	110, 149
14:65	110
14:66–72	92, 111
15:1–15	92, 111–112
15:16–20	92, 112
15:21–22	92, 112–113
15:22	18
15:23–32	92, 113–114
15:33–39	92, 114–116
15:34	18, 115
15:39	114, 146
15:40–41	92, 116
15:42–47	92, 116–117
15:47	132
16:1–8	92, 123–124
16:7	124–125
16:8	116, 124
16:9–20	123

Matthew

1:1–4:6	138
1:1–23	21
1:1	136
1:18–25	21, 22–25
1:20	23
1:23	23
2:1–23	21, 25

158 Index

2:1–12	25–26	13:4–9	37, 46–48
2:1	21	13:10–15	39
2:2–11	22	13:18–23	37, 46–48
2:12	22	13:24–30	18, 37, 48–49
2:13–18	26–27	13:31–32	37, 49–50
2:13–15	22	13:33	37, 49–50
2:16–18	22	13:34–35	18
2:17	18	13:36–43	37, 48–49
2:19–23	22, 27–28	13:27–30	18
2:23	18, 27, 28	13:41	49
		13:44–46	37, 50–51
3:1–4:11	10	13:47–50	18, 37, 48–49
3:7–10	10, 12		
3:17	142	14:22–16:4	11
		14:22–33	58, 72–73
4:–11	12	14:28–31	73
4:3	143	14:32–33	73
4:4	143		
4:6	143	15:21	15
4:7	143		
4:10	143	16:13–28	76, 77–79
4:12–18:35	10	16:16	77
4:12–16	18	16:17–19	78
4:17–16:20	138	16:18	19, 138
		16:21–28:20	138
7:14	23	16:21	117
		16:27	147, 152
8:5–13	12	16:28	18, 118
8:23–27	58, 70–72		
8:20	147	17:1–8	144
8:25	71	17:5	144
8:26	71	17:9	149
8:28	18	17:12	149
8:29	144	17:22	117
9:2–8	10	18:15–17	16
9:3	117	18:17	19
9:6	149		
9:15	117	19:1–20:34	10
10:29–37	11	20:17	117
		20:18	117, 150
11:3	139	20:28	150, 151
11:4–5	140	20:29	19
11:19	147	20:30	140
11:25–27	144		
		21:1–28:20	10
12:8	149	21:1–9	91, 93–94
12:15–21	18	21:10–17	91, 94–95
12:24	117	21:18–19	91, 94

21:20–22	92, 95
21:23–27	92, 95–96
21:33–46	92, 96–97
21:37	145
22:2–7	18
22:7	15
22:15–22	92, 98
22:23–33	92, 98
22:34–40	92, 99–100
22:41–46	92, 100
23:1–36	92
24:27	148
24:30	148
24:37–41	148
24:44	148
25:1–13	18, 37, 51
25:14–30	37, 51–52
25:31–46	18
26:1–5	92, 101
26:6–13	92, 102
26:14–16	92, 102, 106, 117
26:17–19	92, 104
26:20–25	92, 106
26:23	106
26:24	117, 140
26:26–29	92, 106–108
26:26	106
26:28	106
26:30–35	92, 107–108
26:30	106
26:36–46	92, 108–109
26:45	150
26:47–56	92–109
26:56	109
26:57–68	92, 110–111
26:57	110
26:59	110
26:60–61	110
26:63	145
26:64	110, 149
26:67–68	110
26:69–75	92–111
27:1–26	92, 111–112
27:25	112
27:27–31	92, 112
27:32	92, 112–113
27:33–34	92, 113–114
27:45–54	92, 114–116
27:46	114
27:51–53	19
27:54	114
27:55–56	92, 116
27:57–61	92, 116–117
27:61	132
28:1–10	92
28:1–8	122–123
28:9–10	126
28:17	133
28:18–20	19
28:16–20	122, 126–127, 133, 134
28:19	16, 127
28:20	127, 134

Luke

1:1–4	16
1:5–80	20
1:5	21
1:15	20
1:26–38	21, 22–25
1:28	24
1:32	140
1:34–35	24, 116, 142
1:35	20
1:38	24
1:41	20
1:46	20
1:67	20
2:1–52	20
2:1–20	21, 28–31
2:1–5	21
2:1	19
2:6–20	22
2:11–14	94
2:11	138, 152, 153
2:13	29
2:14	20
2:19	30
2:21–40	21, 22, 26, 31–34
2:24	32
2:25–36	20
2:25	138

2:26	138	7:13	68
2:29–32	32	7:15	68
2:29	20	7:17	68
2:32	20	7:19	139
2:34	117	7:22–23	68, 140
2:35	32	7:31	56
2:40	33	7:34	117, 147
2:41–52	21, 33	7:36–50	76, 87–88, 92, 102, 146
2:49	33	7:37	20
		7:42	87
3:1–4:13	10	7:44–45	87
3:1	19	7:47	87, 88
3:6	20	7:48	88
3:7–9	10, 12	7:50	88
3:19	2		
3:22	20, 116, 142	8:1–21	20
		8:3	116
4:1–13	12	8:22–25	58, 70–72
4:1	20	8:25	71
4:3	143	8:26–39	11
4:4	143	8:28	144
4:8	143		
4:10	143	9:22	117, 129, 149
4:12	143	9:26	147, 152
4:14–9:50	10	9:28–36	144
4:16–30	20	9:31	144
4:17–19	46, 116, 129	9:35	144
4:18–19	139	9:44	117, 149
4:18	20, 46	9:51–18:43	10
4:21	139	9:51	117
4:34	144	9:52	20
4:40–41	142	9:58	147
5:12–16	58, 63–64	10:21	20
5:12	153	10:22	144
5:18–26	10	10:25–37	37, 39–40
5:21	117	10:25–28	92, 99–100
5:24	149	10:25	39
5:35	117	110:29	40
		10:30–35	20
6:5	149	10:38–42	20
6:6–11	76, 83–86		
6:11	117	11:5–9	20
6:22	150	11:15	55, 117
		11:37	87
7:1–10	11, 12, 57, 58, 64–65		
7:6–8	65	12:8	148
7:7	65	12:13–21	37, 40–41
7:9	20, 65	12:15	41
7:11–17	58, 68–69	12:19	41
7:11	20	12:40	148

13:10–17	76, 83–86	21:36	148
13:33	117		
		22:1–2	92, 101
14:1–6	76, 83–86	22:1	101
14:1	87	22:2	117
14:3	85	22:3–6	92, 102
14:15	20	22:7–13	92, 104
		22:15–20	92, 106–108
15:1–32	37, 41–43	22:19–20	106, 107
15:1	20	22:21	117
15:17	42	22:21–23	92, 106
15:20	42	22:22	150
15:22	43	22:30	118
15:24	43	22:31–34	92, 107–108
		22:40–46	92, 108–109
17:11–19	58, 63–64	22:43–44	109
17:12	20	22:47–53	92, 109
17:15	64	22:50	117
17:18	64	22:53	109
17:20–21	148	22:54–62	92, 111
17:22–25	148	22:66–71	92, 110, 111
17:26–30	148	22:67–70	111
		22:69	149
18:1–10	9	22:70	145
18:1–8	20		
18:9–14	20, 37, 44	23:1–5	92, 111–112
18:31–33	117, 129	23:2–7	2
18:31	150	23:4	112
18:38	140	23:6–12	112
		23:14	112
19:1–24:53	10	23:17–25	92
19:1–10	20, 76, 88–89, 146	23:22	112
19:10	146, 147	23:25–26	112
19:8	88	23:26–32	92, 112–113
19:9	89	23:33–43	92, 113–114
19:28–38	91, 93–94	23:34	115
19:38	94	23:35	140
19:45–48	91, 94–95	23:39	140
		23:43	115
20:1–8	92, 95–96	23:44–48	92, 114–116
20:9–19	92, 96–97	23:46	20, 115
20:13	145	23:47	114
20:15	145	23:49	92, 116
20:20–26	92, 98	23:50–24:11	20
20:27–40	92, 98	23:50–56	92, 116–117
20:41–44	92, 100	23:55	132
20:45–47	92, 100		
		24:1–11	92, 122–123
21:1–4	20, 92, 100	24:6–7	150
21:20	17	24:6	117
21:27	148	24:7	129

24:12	132	**24:44–49**	130–131
24:13–53	122	**24:46–47**	140
24:13–35	128–129	**24:46**	117, 119, 129
24:26	119, 133, 140	**24:47–49**	133
24:31	133, 134	**24:47**	20, 117, 133
24:36–43	129–130	**24:49**	20, 130
24:41–43	133	**24:50–53**	131
24:42	133	**24:52**	133